Consumerism and Overconsumption

Other Books of Related Interest

Opposing Viewpoints Series

Capitalism
The Corporatization of America
Teens and Social Media

At Issue Series

Food Security
The Media's Influence on Society
The Right to a Living Wage

Current Controversies Series

Fair Trade
The Gig Economy
Sustainable Consumption

> “Congress shall make no law . . . abridging the freedom of speech, or of the press.”
>
> *First Amendment to the U.S. Constitution*

The basic foundation of our democracy is the First Amendment guarantee of freedom of expression. The Opposing Viewpoints series is dedicated to the concept of this basic freedom and the idea that it is more important to practice it than to enshrine it.

Consumerism and Overconsumption

Jennifer Lombardo, Book Editor

Published in 2026 by Greenhaven Publishing, LLC
2544 Clinton Street,
Buffalo NY 14224

First Edition

Articles in Greenhaven Publishing anthologies are often edited for length to meet page requirements. In addition, original titles of these works are changed to clearly present the main thesis and to explicitly indicate the author's opinion. Every effort is made to ensure that Greenhaven Publishing accurately reflects the original intent of the authors. Every effort has been made to trace the owners of the copyrighted material.

Cover image: Jenya Smyk/Shutterstock.com.

Cataloging-in-Publication Data

Names: Lombardo, Jennifer, editor.
Title: Consumerism and overconsumption / edited by Jennifer Lombardo.
Description: First edition. | New York : Greenhaven Publishing,
2026. | Series: Opposing viewpoints | Includes index.
Identifiers: ISBN 9781534510111 (pbk.) | ISBN 9781534510128 (library bound)
Subjects: LCSH: Consumption (Economics)--Juvenile literature. | Consumer goods--Juvenile literature. | Consumer behavior--Juvenile literature. | Economics--Juvenile literature.
Classification: LCC HC79.C6 C66 2026 | DDC 339.47--dc23

Manufactured in the United States of America

Website: http://greenhavenpublishing.com

Contents

The Importance of Opposing Viewpoints 9
Introduction 12

Chapter 1: Is Consumerism Helpful or Harmful to People?

Chapter Preface 16
1. Consumerism Makes People Happier 17
   Steve Quartz
2. Consumerism Does Not Make People Happier 24
   Tori DeAngelis
3. Unneeded Consumption Can Help People Deal with Stress 32
   Jianjia He, Shengmin Liu, Tingting Li, Thi Hoai Thuong Mai
4. Humans Are Not Designed for a Consumerist Society 53
   Yuqian Chang and Kristina M. Durante

Periodical and Internet Sources Bibliography 66

Chapter 2: Who Is Most Responsible for Overconsumption?

Chapter Preface 68
1. People in Wealthy Countries Consume More 69
   Seth Millstein
2. The Rich Are Most Responsible for Overconsumption 79
   Laura Paddison
3. Overpopulation Is Driving Consumption 87
   Natalia Kolkowska
4. Corporations Push Overconsumption 95
   Niloufar Fallah Shayan, Nasrin Mohabbati-Kalejahi, Sepideh Alavi, andMohammad Ali Zahed

Periodical and Internet Sources Bibliography 103

Chapter 3: Can We Solve the Problem of Overconsumption?

Chapter Preface 105

1. Greenwashing Is Part of the Problem 106
   United Nations
2. Economic Growth Is as Important as Environmentalism 112
   Steven Cohen
3. We All Need to Be Conscious Consumers 119
   Olwen van Dijk-Hildebrand

Periodical and Internet Sources Bibliography 124

Chapter 4: Is Consumerism without Overconsumption Possible?

Chapter Preface 126

1. To Stop Overconsuming, We Must Stop Shopping 127
   Jamie Waters
2. A Circular Economy Is Not Easy to Implement 135
   Lea Becker Frahm, Casper Boks, and Linda Nhu Laursen
3. A Circular Economy Is Crucial to Reducing Consumption 155
   Heinrich Böll Foundation
4. A Circular Economy Is Not Easy to Implement 135
   Lea Becker Frahm, Casper Boks, and Linda Nhu Laursen

Periodical and Internet Sources Bibliography 167

For Further Discussion 168

Organizations to Contact 169

Bibliography of Books 172

Index 173

The Importance of Opposing Viewpoints

Perhaps every generation experiences a period in time in which the populace seems especially polarized, starkly divided on the important issues of the day and gravitating toward the far ends of the political spectrum and away from a consensus-facilitating middle ground. The world that today's students are growing up in and that they will soon enter into as active and engaged citizens is deeply fragmented in just this way. Issues relating to terrorism, immigration, women's rights, minority rights, race relations, health care, taxation, wealth and poverty, the environment, policing, military intervention, the proper role of government—in some ways, perennial issues that are freshly and uniquely urgent and vital with each new generation—are currently roiling the world.

If we are to foster a knowledgeable, responsible, active, and engaged citizenry among today's youth, we must provide them with the intellectual, interpretive, and critical-thinking tools and experience necessary to make sense of the world around them and of the all-important debates and arguments that inform it. After all, the outcome of these debates will in large measure determine the future course, prospects, and outcomes of the world and its peoples, particularly its youth. If they are to become successful members of society and productive and informed citizens, students need to learn how to evaluate the strengths and weaknesses of someone else's arguments, how to sift fact from opinion and fallacy, and how to test the relative merits and validity of their own opinions against the known facts and the best possible available information. The landmark series Opposing Viewpoints has been providing students with just such critical-thinking skills and exposure to the debates surrounding society's most urgent contemporary issues for many years, and it continues to serve this essential role with undiminished commitment, care, and rigor.

The key to the series's success in achieving its goal of sharpening students' critical-thinking and analytic skills resides in its title—

Opposing Viewpoints. In every intriguing, compelling, and engaging volume of this series, readers are presented with the widest possible spectrum of distinct viewpoints, expert opinions, and informed argumentation and commentary, supplied by some of today's leading academics, thinkers, analysts, politicians, policy makers, economists, activists, change agents, and advocates. Every opinion and argument anthologized here is presented objectively and accorded respect. There is no editorializing in any introductory text or in the arrangement and order of the pieces. No piece is included as a "straw man," an easy ideological target for cheap point-scoring. As wide and inclusive a range of viewpoints as possible is offered, with no privileging of one particular political ideology or cultural perspective over another. It is left to each individual reader to evaluate the relative merits of each argument—as they see it, and with the use of ever-growing critical-thinking skills—and grapple with their own assumptions, beliefs, and perspectives to determine how convincing or successful any given argument is and how the reader's own stance on the issue may be modified or altered in response to it.

This process is facilitated and supported by volume, chapter, and selection introductions that provide readers with the essential context they need to begin engaging with the spotlighted issues, with the debates surrounding them, and with their own perhaps shifting or nascent opinions on them. In addition, guided reading and discussion questions encourage readers to determine the authors' point of view and purpose, interrogate and analyze the various arguments and their rhetoric and structure, evaluate the arguments' strengths and weaknesses, test their claims against available facts and evidence, judge the validity of the reasoning, and bring into clearer, sharper focus the reader's own beliefs and conclusions and how they may differ from or align with those in the collection or those of their classmates.

Research has shown that reading comprehension skills improve dramatically when students are provided with compelling, intriguing, and relevant "discussable" texts. The subject matter of these collections could not be more compelling, intriguing, or urgently relevant to today's students and the world they are poised to inherit. The anthologized articles and the reading and discussion questions that are included with them also provide the basis for stimulating, lively, and passionate classroom debates. Students who are compelled to anticipate objections to their own argument and identify the flaws in those of an opponent read more carefully, think more critically, and steep themselves in relevant context, facts, and information more thoroughly. In short, using discussable text of the kind provided by every single volume in the Opposing Viewpoints series encourages close reading, facilitates reading comprehension, fosters research, strengthens critical thinking, and greatly enlivens and energizes classroom discussion and participation. The entire learning process is deepened, extended, and strengthened.

For all of these reasons, Opposing Viewpoints continues to be exactly the right resource at exactly the right time—when we most need to provide readers with the critical-thinking tools and skills that will not only serve them well in school but also in their careers and their daily lives as decision-making family members, community members, and citizens. This series encourages respectful engagement with and analysis of opposing viewpoints and fosters a resulting increase in the strength and rigor of one's own opinions and stances. As such, it helps make readers "future ready," and that readiness will pay rich dividends for the readers themselves, for the citizenry, for our society, and for the world at large.

Introduction

> *"Overconsumption is the mother of all environmental problems. For the first time in the history of capitalism, consumption itself has become controversial."*
>
> — *Kalle Lasn*

In today's world, consumerism is more than a feature of modern life; for many people, it is the defining framework of their identities, relationships, and aspirations. We live in a society shaped by what we buy, how much we buy, and how quickly we replace it. People buy things to fill their homes, entertain themselves, and sometimes even give them a sense of self-worth. For some people, shopping is a necessity; for others, it is a form of entertainment, self-expression, or even emotional coping. The push toward consumerism seems to be everywhere: How many teen movies feature a shopping spree in a mall? How many adult TV shows have characters engage in "retail therapy" when they encounter challenges in life? How many ads do we encounter in any given day?

Supporters of consumerism argue that this system fuels progress. They point out that consumer demand drives innovation, competition, and economic growth. In market-driven economies, purchasing power gives individuals freedom and agency. They say that consumers can choose the products and services that best suit their needs, and businesses, in turn, are motivated to improve quality, efficiency, and affordability. From this perspective, the rise of global consumer culture is a triumph of access and abundance. It reflects the success of modern capitalism in lifting millions out of poverty, creating jobs, and expanding choices.

However, critics tell a different story. They warn that consumerism often leads to overconsumption—using far more than any single person needs, and certainly more than the planet can sustainably provide. Critics argue that this lifestyle contributes to environmental degradation, climate change, and the exploitation of both human labor and natural resources. Overconsumption, they say, doesn't just harm the environment—it also harms individuals by fostering materialism, stress, and a constant sense of dissatisfaction. Many believe that the pursuit of "more" can distract from deeper values like community, creativity, and well-being.

The debate becomes even more urgent in the context of global inequality. While some nations experience a surplus of goods, others struggle with scarcity. Critics of consumerism ask whether it is ethical for a small percentage of the world's population to consume the majority of its resources. At the same time, developing nations are often encouraged—or pressured—to adopt the same consumption patterns that industrialized countries have long followed, raising questions about justice, sustainability, and cultural identity.

Technology and media also play a major role. Advertising is more sophisticated and targeted than ever before, often encouraging impulsive spending and unrealistic ideals. Social media platforms can amplify the pressure to "keep up," pushing people to present curated lifestyles built around possessions and appearances. In this environment, it becomes harder to distinguish between genuine desire and manufactured demand.

Is consumerism empowering or exploitative? Is overconsumption an individual failing or a systemic issue? Should we embrace minimalism and responsible consumption, or is that a privileged ideal available only to a few? These are the questions at the heart of the issue.

This volume presents a range of viewpoints on the complex and often controversial topics of consumerism and overconsumption. Various articles and studies taken from various sources examine how consumer culture affects the world and what alternatives, if any, might exist. In doing so, this volume encourages critical thinking, informed dialogue, and a deeper understanding of the forces shaping how we live today.

Chapter 1

Is Consumerism Helpful or Harmful to People?

Chapter Preface

Consumerism is often seen as a symbol of freedom and success, especially in cultures such as the United States. Proponents of capitalism see consumerism as proof that individuals can choose what they want, when they want it. From smartphones to fashion, the ability to buy and own things has become deeply tied to personal identity and social status. For many, consumer culture brings convenience, variety, and the thrill of new experiences.

However, not everyone sees consumerism in a positive light. Critics note that although people in many parts of the world have access today to more money and more material goods than at any previous point in history, rates of mental illnesses such as depression and anxiety are rising. Some people believe this is a direct result of the pressure to earn and consume more; others believe that consumerism simply does not make us as happy as its supporters say.

By presenting a range of arguments, this chapter invites readers to reflect on their own experiences as consumers and to consider whether engaging in consumerism is helpful, harmful, or simply an experience that is shaped by the consumer themselves.

Viewpoint 1

> *"... if material welfare, purchasing power, and happiness are indeed strongly linked — then the anti-consumer view and its conception of consumerism as an irrational status zero-sum contest must be fundamentally flawed."*

Consumerism Makes People Happier

Steve Quartz

"Retail therapy" is a longstanding trope suggesting that when someone is down in the dumps, they will feel better if they go shopping, even if they do not need anything specific. Critics of this practice suggest that people who engage in it are shallow and materialistic. However, in this viewpoint, Steve Quartz suggests that engaging in consumerism meets a psychological need that boosts people's sense of wellbeing. Steve Quartz is a professor of philosophy and neuroscience at the California Institute of Technology and co-author of the book Cool: How the Brain's Hidden Quest for Cool Drives Our Economy and Shapes Our World.

As you read, consider the following questions:

1. What research made people question the Easterlin Paradox?
2. How do you feel when you buy something new?

"Why buying things makes you happy" by Steve Quartz, News Hour Productions, September 9, 2015. Reprinted by permission.

3. What is the relationship between material wealth and social status?

From pop songs to Pope Francis, consumerism is often denounced as a poison that thwarts genuine happiness, hampers political participation and erodes social connections. Even many consumer theorists suspect that motives like envy and a hunger to emulate higher-ups drives our consumption. Pointing the finger at an insatiable thirst for status, critics argue that our pursuit of "stuff" locks us in an irrational consumer arms race, where we compete for status through ever more wasteful purchases.

For over 40 years, some economists and anti-consumerists have pointed to a series of findings dubbed "The Easterlin Paradox" as the incriminating evidence that our increasing consumption makes us no happier. In 1974, Richard Easterlin reported that although richer people were happier than poorer people in the same country, people in wealthier countries were no happier than those in poorer ones. The implication was that happiness depended on relative income—how we stack up against the proverbial Joneses. Imagine if we doubled everyone's income overnight. It would have no effect on your ability to keep up with the Joneses since theirs doubled as well. Just as all the children of Lake Wobegon can't really be above average—at least compared to each other—status, like rank in a Lake Wobegon classroom, is all relative. The only way to gain status is by someone else losing some—it's a zero-sum contest. If only the Joneses would stop buying bigger houses and fancier cars…

But new studies question whether there ever was an Easterlin Paradox. The 2006 Gallop World Poll, which included nationally representative surveys from 132 countries, was the first erosion to the concept. In 2008, economist Angus Deaton found a strong global relationship between a country's wealth (Gross Domestic Product per capita) and happiness (measured by life satisfaction). As he noted, the people of sub-Saharan Africa are not as satisfied with their lives as people in India, who are not as satisfied with their lives as the people of France or Denmark.

It seemed like many psychologists, sociologists and culture critics were studying consumerism from the armchair with more interest in condemning it than understanding it.

Deaton found no evidence for an idea that had become lore in the field and a mantra among anti-consumers: that once a country's wealth satisfied its citizens' basic needs, more wealth doesn't increase happiness. Examining subsequent waves of the Gallop World Poll, now including 155 countries, economists Betsey Stevenson and Justin Wolfers similarly found a global relationship between income and life satisfaction. Recently, the psychologist Ed Diener, a pioneer in the scientific study of happiness, found that using household income instead of the more indirect measure of GDP per capita revealed even stronger links between material welfare, purchasing power and happiness that were long enduring.

If there's no paradox—if material welfare, purchasing power, and happiness are indeed strongly linked—then the anti-consumer view and its conception of consumerism as an irrational status zero-sum contest must be fundamentally flawed.

A decade ago, cracks in the Easterlin Paradox were causing me to wonder if my own anti-consumer intuitions were ill-founded. When I turned to examine consumer theories, I found much of the research deeply tinged with strong moral overtones. It seemed like many psychologists, sociologists and culture critics were studying consumerism from the armchair with more interest in condemning it than understanding it. To try to better understand why we consume, I started to develop a "consumer neuroscience" that I hoped would answer some of these mysteries by tapping into the unconscious brain processes underlying our purchase decisions. At the time, brain imaging was opening a new window into the workings of the mind, and I suspected looking at these processes, rather than relying just on people's introspection, would provide a clearer foundation for a theory of our consumer behavior.

In one experiment, my colleagues and I were interested in probing why entire industries, from running shoes (think Air Jordan) to computers (think Mac), depended on how people perceived their products as cool or not. Most of the products we use are infused with symbolic meanings, cool among them, which adds value to them beyond their functionality. As the anthropologist Daniel Miller has long studied, humans have long used the symbolic meaning of the stuff around us, our material culture, to create our social identity and define our social relationships.

We found that asking people to merely look at products they considered "cool" sparked a pattern of activation in a part of the brain known as the medial prefrontal cortex. The activation was similar to what we see when people receive a compliment or feel valued by others, that is, when their perceived status increases. Even more interesting was the fact that this part of the brain had expanded the most during human evolution. This expansion gave rise to our capacity for self-reflection and to think about others in terms of their thoughts and feelings. These are all critical social capacities that allow us to build our complex social worlds. It was a captivating convergence to find such symbiosis between our expanded medial prefrontal cortex, which gives rise to our social selves, and the material culture we build, which helps define and shape our social identity.

The medial prefrontal cortex also creates social emotions that are likely uniquely human, particularly the positive emotions we feel when others value us, such as pride, and the strongly aversive emotions we feel when we think others think poorly of us, such as shame and guilt. These create the basic motivations that drive us to affiliate with others and ultimately to use our patterns of consumption to help create the social groups.

Understanding how products impact us in light of our brain's evolutionary history compels us to rethink many of our most basic assumptions about why we consume. The complex emotional life our medial prefrontal cortex creates gives rise to our most basic social impulses: to form intimate partnerships, friendships and alliances—to create the groups through which we gain our sense of belonging. During evolution, one's life success was critically tied to the quality of partners and alliances one made. This is true today. An extraordinary amount of our social behavior revolves around seeking out and maintaining romantic partnerships and friendships, an evolutionary pressure known as social selection.

Social selection has created deep-seated needs in us to display our value as social partners through acts of generosity, kindness and understanding of social norms. Evolutionary biologists describe these as costly signals of our trustworthiness and worth as a partner and friend. Virtually every social behavior contains some signaling element that conveys something about us to others, from how we walk to how we talk to how we eat. The latest Emily Post etiquette book comes in at a back-breaking 865 pages—a testimony to the extraordinarily complex symbolic layers of our social life.

It now appears that the very first signs of our humanity dawned when our ancestors began using the material around them in this symbolic way—the very first shell necklaces some 70,000 years ago might have symbolized membership in a group or perhaps some social role within that group. Today, our patterns of consumption draw on these very same affiliative roots, as we use products to convey who we are to others.

We can do this because our medial prefrontal cortex works as a sort of social calculator that monitors our perceptions of other people's judgments of us, a sort of self-esteem inner gauge. It creates our basic need to feel the face-to-face admiration and respect we obtain in groups. In fact, psychologists have discovered that our happiness depends more on this feeling of esteem and respect than on our socioeconomic status. That's because seeking esteem through our patterns of consumption is a relatively recent cultural invention, tracing back to 18th century England. For most of our species' existence, status came in non-economic forms, including social networks, physical strength and practical skills and knowledge.

What all this suggests is that our modern patterns of consumption tap into this more basic need for social esteem, which drives us to create social groups around common values and norms. Today, we call these consumer lifestyles consumer tribes, brand communities or consumption microcultures. Most consumer products are potent social signals, which people use to signal, often unconsciously, their values to others. Few people would drive a Prius to a NASCAR race while fewer still would drive a Hummer to an environmental meeting. A hippie would rather walk than drive a BMW. Consumer researchers have found that people bond over these shared preferences, with common patterns of consumption defining and shaping their social groups.

In fact, much of the economic value of products today lies in their impact on our brain's mostly implicit estimate of how they impact our social identity. In collaboration with Read Montague's lab at Baylor College of Medicine, we found that boosts in our social status also strongly activate the nucleus accumbens, a critical part of the brain's reward system that's implicated in almost all forms of addiction. Other studies with college students found that they value self-esteem boosts even more than sex!

But I would urge you not to view these as some misbegotten vanity. Feeling esteemed and respected by others is a basic and universal human need that makes possible the human bonds that underlie cooperative human social life. It's no surprise that it taps into the brain's most powerful reward systems.

Viewed in this light, I think a good way of thinking about consumerism is as a way of converting income into the lifestyles that allow us to create and engage in diverse social groups that satisfy our need to belong and to feel respected, esteemed and valued by others. That's why our incomes won't have their full impact on our happiness unless we convert some of them into status. While many status systems that aren't connected to economic life still exist, status is typically in extremely limited supply in traditional societies that do not use consumerism as a way of supplying status. And it's also typically reserved for a ruling elite.

The Easterlin Paradox assumed that status seeking was a zero-sum contest. If the total amount of status or esteem is fixed, then the only way to get more of it is by someone losing some of theirs. As I explore tomorrow, this also turns out to be false. In the 1950s, something happened to how we consume, which allowed new forms of status to emerge, helping to solve a critically important but under appreciated social problem: if our happiness depends on attaining esteem and the respect of others through participating in social groups, how can a society meet that demand?

> *"People with strong materialistic values appear to have goal orientations that may lead to poorer well-being ..."*

Consumerism Does Not Make People Happier

Tori DeAngelis

Despite the wealth gap that exists within the country, the United States is one of the richest countries in the world. More objects are available for purchase than existed less than a century ago, and Americans today generally have more money to spend than their ancestors did. Does all of this wealth make us happier than people were a century ago? In this article published by the American Psychological Association, writer Tori DeAngelis argues that it does not.

As you read, consider the following questions:

1. How can consumerism negatively affect mental health and happiness?
2. Is there a difference between materialism and consumerism?
3. How can people maximize their happiness in a materialist society?

Compared with Americans in 1957, today we own twice as many cars per person, eat out twice as often and enjoy endless other commodities that weren't around then - big-screen TVs, microwave ovens, SUVs and handheld wireless devices, to name a few. But are we any happier?

Certainly, happiness is difficult to pin down, let alone measure. But a recent literature review suggests we're no more contented than we were then—in fact, maybe less so.

"Compared with their grandparents, today's young adults have grown up with much more affluence, slightly less happiness and much greater risk of depression and assorted social pathology," notes Hope College psychologist David G. Myers, PhD, author of the article, which appeared in the *American Psychologist* (Vol. 55, No. 1). "Our becoming much better off over the last four decades has not been accompanied by one iota of increased subjective well-being."

These findings emerge at a time when the consumer culture has reached a fever pitch, comments Myers, also the author of "The American Paradox: Spiritual Hunger in an Age of Plenty" (Yale University Press, 2000).

So what does psychologists' research say about possible effects of this consumer culture on people's mental well-being? Based on the literature to date, it would be too simplistic to say that desire for material wealth unequivocally means discontent. Although the least materialistic people report the most life satisfaction, some studies indicate that materialists can be almost as contented if they've got the money and their acquisitive lifestyle doesn't conflict with more soul-satisfying pursuits. But for materialists with less money and other conflicting desires—a more common situation—unhappiness emerges, researchers are finding.

"There's a narrowing of the gap between materialists and nonmaterialists in life satisfaction as materialists' income rises," notes Edward Diener, PhD, a well-known researcher of subjective well-being and materialism at the University of

Illinois at Urbana-Champaign. "So if you're poor, it's very bad to be a materialist; and if you're rich, it doesn't make you happier than nonmaterialists, but you almost catch up."

Why are materialists unhappy?

As with all things psychological, the relationship between mental state and materialism is complex: Indeed, researchers are still trying to ascertain whether materialism stokes unhappiness, unhappiness fuels materialism, or both. Diener suggests that several factors may help explain the apparent toll of pursuit of wealth. In simple terms, a strong consumerist bent—what William Wordsworth in 1807 called "getting and spending"—can promote unhappiness because it takes time away from the things that can nurture happiness, including relationships with family and friends, research shows.

"It's not absolutely necessary that chasing after material wealth will interfere with your social life," Diener says. "But it can, and if it does, it probably has a net negative payoff in terms of life satisfaction and well-being."

People with strong materialistic values appear to have goal orientations that may lead to poorer well-being, adds Knox College psychologist Tim Kasser, PhD, who with Berkeley, Calif., psychotherapist Allen Kanner, PhD, co-edited a new APA book, "Psychology and Consumer Culture" (APA, 2004), featuring experts' research and views on the links between consumerism, well-being and environmental and social factors.

In Kasser's own book, "The High Price of Materialism" (MIT Press, 2002), Kasser describes his and others' research showing that when people organize their lives around extrinsic goals such as product acquisition, they report greater unhappiness in relationships, poorer moods and more psychological problems. Kasser distinguishes extrinsic goals—which tend to focus on possessions, image, status and receiving rewards and praise—from intrinsic ones, which aim at outcomes like personal growth and community connection and are satisfying in and of themselves.

Relatedly, a not-yet-published study by University of Missouri social psychologist Marsha Richins, PhD, finds that materialists place unrealistically high expectations on what consumer goods can do for them in terms of relationships, autonomy and happiness.

"They think that having these things is going to change their lives in every possible way you can think of," she says. One man in Richins's study, for example, said he desperately wanted a swimming pool so he could improve his relationship with his moody 13-year-old daughter.

The roots of materialism

Given that we all experience the same consumeristic culture, why do some of us develop strongly materialistic values and others don't? A line of research suggests that insecurity—both financial and emotional—lies at the heart of consumeristic cravings. Indeed, it's not money per se, but the striving for it, that's linked to unhappiness, find Diener and others.

"Research suggests that when people grow up in unfortunate social situations--where they're not treated very nicely by their parents or when they experience poverty or even the threat of death," says Kasser, "they become more materialistic as a way to adapt."

A 1995 paper in *Developmental Psychology* (Vol. 31, No. 6) by Kasser and colleagues was the first to demonstrate this. Teens who reported having higher materialistic attitudes tended to be poorer and to have less nurturing mothers than those with lower materialism scores, the team found. Similarly, a 1997 study in the *Journal of Consumer Research* (Vol. 23, No. 4) headed up by Aric Rindfleisch, PhD, then a doctoral student at the University of Wisconsin-Madison and now an associate professor of marketing there, found that young people whose parents were undergoing or had undergone divorce or separation were more prone to developing materialistic values later in life than those from intact homes.

And in the first direct experimental test of the point, Kasser and University of Missouri social psychologist Kenneth Sheldon, PhD, reported in a 2000 article in Psychological Science (Vol. 11, No. 4), that when provoked with thoughts of the most extreme uncertainty of them all—death—people reported more materialistic leanings.

More money = greater happiness?

The ill effects of materialism appear subject to modification, other research finds. In a longitudinal study reported in the November 2003 issue of *Psychological Science* (Vol. 14, No. 6), psychologists Carol Nickerson, PhD, of the University of Illinois at Urbana-Champaign, Norbert Schwarz, PhD, of the University of Michigan, Diener, and Daniel Kahnemann, PhD, of Princeton University, examined two linked data sets collected 19 years apart on 12,000 people who had attended elite colleges and universities in the 1970s—one drawn in 1976 when they were freshmen, the other in 1995.

On average, those who had initially expressed stronger financial aspirations reported lower life satisfaction two decades later than those expressing lower monetary desires. But as the income of the higher-aspiration participants rose, so did their reported life satisfaction, the team found.

James E. Burroughs, PhD, assistant professor of commerce at the University of Virginia's McIntire School of Commerce, and the University of Wisconsin's Rindfleisch conclude that the unhappiest materialists are those whose materialistic and higher-order values are most conflicted. In a 2002 paper in the *Journal of Consumer Research* (Vol. 29, No. 3), the team first gauged people's levels of stress, materialistic values and prosocial values in the domains of family, religion and community—in keeping with the theory of psychologist Shalom Schwartz, PhD, that some values unavoidably conflict with one another. Then in an experimental study, they ascertained the degree of conflict people felt when making a decision between the two value domains.

The unhappiest people were those with the most conflict--those who reported high prosocial and high materialistic values, says Burroughs. The other three groups—those low in materialism and high in prosocial values, those low in prosocial values and high in materialism, and those lukewarm in both arenas—reported similar, but lower levels of life stress.

His findings square with those of others: that the differences in life satisfaction between more and less materialistic people are relatively small, says Burroughs. And most researchers in the area agree that these values lie along a continuum, he adds.

"Material things are neither bad nor good," Burroughs comments. "It is the role and status they are accorded in one's life that can be problematic. The key is to find a balance: to appreciate what you have, but not at the expense of the things that really matter—your family, community and spirituality."

The bigger picture

Even if some materialists swim through life with little distress, however, consumerism carries larger costs that are worth worrying about, others say. "There are consequences of materialism that can affect the quality of other people's and other species' lives," says Kasser.

To that end, he and others are beginning to study links between materialistic values and attitudes toward the environment, and to write about the way consumerism has come to affect our collective psyche. Psychotherapist Kanner, who co-edited "Psychology and Consumer Culture" with Kasser, cites examples as minor as parents who "outsource" parental activities like driving their children to school and those as big as international corporations leading people in poor countries to crave products they can ill afford.

Indeed, consumerism is an example of an area where psychology needs to stretch from its focus on the individual and examine the wider impact of the phenomenon, Kanner believes.

"Corporate-driven consumerism is having massive psychological effects, not just on people, but on our planet as well," he says. "Too often, psychology over-individualizes social problems. In so doing, we end up blaming the victim, in this instance by locating materialism primarily in the person while ignoring the huge corporate culture that's invading so much of our lives."

Pros and Cons of Consumerism

Consumerism is an economic theory that consumer spending is the key to individual well-being and the most important factor driving a country's economic growth. Consumerist societies measure their economic success through their gross domestic product (GDP), and consumer spending effectively increases that number. Capitalist economies depend on the consumption of goods and encourage their populations to purchase beyond their basic needs to keep the economy thriving.

How Does Consumerism Work?

Consumerism works by creating an economic system that encourages consumers to buy more through social pressure, advertising, manipulation, and the belief that you'll be happier if you own a particular item.

...

5 Pros of Consumerism

Experts debate whether consumerism benefits or hurts societal ways of life. Some possible advantages of consumerism include:

1. Creates jobs: Producing new products and services through consumerism requires workers. In theory, the more successful companies that grow out of consumerism, the more jobs created for civilians.
2. Encourages innovation: If your company does well, you'll most likely want to expand. Expansion means innovation, creativity, and the funds to support your new goals.
3. Ensures quality: Because companies compete with one another for your business, producing high-quality material goods at a competitive price should serve their goals.

4. Promotes fair prices and consumer choice: Companies compete with one another for customers in a capitalist society. Consumerism creates a market with multiple options, allowing you to search for the best price for similar products.
5. Stimulates economic growth: You can think of consumerism as a merry-go-round where manufacturers create a product and everyone buys it, which increases demand, forcing manufacturers to develop more of the product. The process theoretically allows the economy to grow through more jobs, better wages, increased spending, and a rise in the gross domestic product.

4 Cons of Consumerism

Experts argue that consumerism negatively affects society and contributes to the degradation of traditional ways of life. Drawbacks of consumerism include:

1. Consumer exploitation: Consumerism depends on your desire to buy things, even if it hurts you financially or psychologically to do so. It encourages reflexive consumption and an association between purchasing something and your happiness.
2. Creates class barriers: Consumerism, specifically conspicuous consumption, reinforces class barriers by creating a divide between those who can afford nice things and those who cannot. Learn more about income inequality with economist Paul Krugman.
3. Negative impact on the environment: Consumerism affects natural resources through overproduction. These behaviors lead to draining natural resources to extinction and creating pollution that damages the environment and leads to climate change.
4. Wasteful: Disposable products and planned obsolescence mean people are buying new versions of the same things repeatedly, creating an abundance of waste.

"Consumerism Definition: Examples, Pros and Cons" by MasterClass, August 9, 2022.

Viewpoint 3

> "When ... consumers engage in unneeded consumption behaviour, they may improve their mood by satisfying the psychological needs that the acquisition of necessities might not meet."

Unneeded Consumption Can Help People Deal with Stress

Jianjia He, Shengmin Liu, Tingting Li, Thi Hoai Thuong Mai

In a capitalist society, buying at least some items is unavoidable. However, many people buy much more than they strictly need. Sometimes, as with toilet paper in the beginning of the COVID-19 pandemic, they do this out of fear that the item will not be available later. Other times, people simply buy more than they need because it is a luxury to be able to do so. Jianjia He, Shengmin Liu, Tingting Li, and Thi Hoai Thuong Mai conducted a study that suggests this type of unneeded consumption helped people deal with the stress they felt during the pandemic. The four authors are researchers at the Business School, University of Shanghai for Science and Technology in Shanghai, China.

"The Positive Effects of Unneeded Consumption Behaviour on Consumers during the COVID-19 Pandemic" by He J, Liu S, Li T and Mai THT, National Library of Medicine, June 13, 2021.

As you read, consider the following questions:

1. How is unneeded consumption different than panic buying?
2. What other stressful events might lead someone to buy things they don't need?
3. What are the benefits and drawbacks of unneeded consumption?

Introduction

During the COVID-19 pandemic and community lockdown, most workers had to work from home, and their consumption choices were limited. At times, they would be permitted a brief amount of time to purchase necessary products and would often buy unnecessary items. Why have these phenomena spread in the nationwide lockdown during the COVID-19 pandemic?

Unneeded consumption is a kind of state when consumers buy more products than they require [1]. For example, one consumer needs forty pieces of bread to eat in 10 days; however, fifty pieces of bread is purchased even though the bread quality guarantee is ten days. Thus, ten pieces of bread are classed as unnecessary consumption. Unneeded consumption aims to satisfy psychological desires, where the main focus is on the consumption of material possessions to achieve the value of psychological well-being. Income, stress and consumption habit may influence the vary of unneeded consumption [2,3,4]. For example, consumers may neglect the quantities needed when they buy their favourite goods. A consumer wants to enjoy the purchasing process to relieve stress despite their budget and the necessary quantities required as high income and consumption inertia is in effect.

A similar topic that is a feature of crisis-related insecurity is panic buying and stockpiling behaviour, with such related behaviour being a widely reported response to COVID-19 intervention measures enacted by the government

[5,6,7]. Understanding such purchasing and stockpiling behaviour is essential for the disaster management sector and retail organisations [8].

Unneeded consumption is different from panic buying. Panic buying is caused by the object of acquiring security and preparing for future needs [9]. Unneeded consumption is activated by the habitual trend or relieving stress after lockdown [3,4,5]. Panic buying is anchoring on the shelf of markets but unneeded consumption anchors on consumers' basic needs. Panic buying shows consumers buy out of the shelf on the market but unneeded consumption only means that the quantities of goods they buy exceed consumers' necessary quantities from basic needs. The direct factor of unneeded consumption may be pressed in lockdown for a long time and consumers need to relieve their pressed motive by engaging in unneeded consumption. Unneeded consumers do not consider whether or not the goods they buy is useful for the future, which is different from panic buying. Unneeded consumption happens with their habitual inertia or relieving their stress, not with planning intention to hoarding or stockpiling, which is the act of collecting and safeguarding a large number of possessions for future use [10].

Unneeded consumption of goods and services increases the use of natural resources that is a major cause of environmental problems, including global warming, polluted air and water and biodiversity reduction [11]. Unneeded consumption also results in producing more packaging material that must be disposed of. On the other hands, previous scholars have found many inhibitors to minimise redundant consumption [12]. Unnecessary consumption behaviours could be limited through the promotion of social responsibility or self-control trends [1]. Meanwhile, such behaviours positively influence psychological well-being or happiness [13,14]. More specifically, unneeded consumption in a home environment is seen as a tool to connect family members during the COVID-19 pandemic. According to

Bahagia et al. [15], in this pandemic, most homemakers have to face many challenges such as supervising their children while doing house chores. Further, some may be working from home and considered an invisible pressure from the family aspect, therefore buying more than they need is a way to reduce stress during social distancing. However, why has such behaviour arisen during the COVID-19 pandemic? Does engaging in unneeded consumption behaviour have a positive effect on consumers (workers)?

Previous studies have focused on the detriments of unneeded consumption behaviour on the environment and demonstrated emotional regulation strategies used by consumers in surplus purchasing [14]. Specifically, surplus purchasing can be reappraised according to the emotions experienced in the purchasing process. For example, assuming that somebody likes bread and would like to buy one bread for their dinner. After the purchasing process, they can recognise that the quantity of bread they have purchased is more than their basic need. The reason is in the purchasing process: they will experience the positive emotion, as in the hedonic motivation of impulse buying [16], and reappraise the benefits of such behaviour, to experience positive emotions on the spot, which improves consumers' recovery level [17,18]. If consumers experience high levels of recovery from unneeded consumption behaviour, what is the subsequent outcome?

During the COVID-19 pandemic, more consumers worked from home as both consumers and employees; they needed a way to recover from their psychological resources because of the burden of additional stressors such as individual isolation and fear of COVID-19, which made it difficult to engage in their work due to frequent interruptions in the form of community lockdowns and daily virus detection. If consumers experience positive emotions and recovery in unneeded consumption behaviour, would they direct these psychological benefits to their work roles and improve their engagement? If so, when would this shift occur?

To answer these questions, we built a moderated mediating model to explore the positive influence of unneeded consumption behaviour on work engagement via the shift of recovery level from life to the workplace. The COVID-19 pandemic has caused many psychological injuries for most people, and they need a way to replenish themselves. Individual coping and self-regulation are related to explaining individual responses or reactions to emerging stressors from the COVID-19 pandemic [19]. The conservation of resources theory (COR) can explain how these workers/consumers cope with these stressors (unneeded consumption behaviour-recover-engagement). Further, the individualism-collectivism cultural perspective was used to explore when unneeded consumption behaviour is positive.

Addressing the repairing function of indulgence [20] in the individualism value, we chose consumer indulgence as a positive mediator between unneeded consumption behaviour and work engagement. Based on the effects of responsibility reminders [1] in the collectivism value, perceived consumer effectiveness was considered as the negative mediator in the hypothetical model.

Theoretical Framework

The COVID-19 pandemic emerged as a traumatic event that required people to make sense of the situation and choose appropriate reactions. Culture plays an important role in shaping the way individuals assess or cope with stressors related to the COVID-19 pandemic. Further, there are huge cross-cultural differences in individuals' appraisals of stressors, choices of coping strategies and indicators of adaptive outcomes [21]. Since cultural values show the desirable end states that ought to be pursued [22,23,24] they tend to shape members' attentiveness to or prioritisation of stressors in relation to appraisal processes.

Individuals in this study are from the same nation and are socialised to use their culture-specific orientations to guide their daily coping processes. For example, in China where the culture values collectivism (vs. individualism), people tend to form an interdependent (vs. independent) self-construal [25] and prefer to use ought self (vs. ideal self) to guide their behaviours. Obeying government rules on limiting travel, most Chinese employees work at home and schedule times to buy products in the supermarket. Buying products in a supermarket is an opportunity to release their stress during this pandemic. Unneeded consumption often occurs because consumers consider unneeded products can be potentially effective for their family members using interdependent value. Furthermore, an unneeded consumption process can be a positive recovery factor to help release stress after nationwide lockdown and individual insolation. According to the lockdown rules in China, the government permits only one person from a family to buy products outside of the home, therefore, it can be difficult to know all needs of their family members. Thus, unneeded products may be purchased to satisfy family members' potential needs.

Unneeded consumption behaviour is considered "redundant shopping" [26]. Why do consumers expend their economic resources to buy unnecessary products? When these consumers engage in unneeded consumption behaviour, they may improve their mood [20] by satisfying the psychological needs that the acquisition of necessities might not meet [27]. Such unneeded consumption behaviour fluctuates daily and such fluctuations always coincide with changes in resource conservation and generation [28]. Thus, the conservation of resources theory (COR) may explain the proximal actor-based effects of daily, unneeded consumption behaviour. The COR describes how individuals strive to retain, acquire and attain resources and decrease the threat of net resource loss. In particular, according to COR, people tend to minimise net loss when they are confronted with stress [29]. The theory reveals the regulated process of resources according to the behavioural stress they are experiencing. Stress refers to the reaction to the environment where there is a threat of resource loss, net resource loss, or a lack of opportunities to gain resources; resources include energy, conditions, personal characteristics and anything needed to attain goals [30,31]. A primary understanding of resource loss promotes the idea that losing direct resources is more harmful than gaining the resources that were lost [31].

The present study focuses on the proximal positive effects of unneeded consumption behaviour for actors. From the perspective of resource conservation, there are certain reasons why unneeded consumption behaviour may help consumers avoid loss. Many utilitarian consumption behaviour activities include controlling resources to satisfy basic needs [32]. For example, consumers purchase necessary products at first and buy unnecessary products through buying inertia if they do not control their budget and purchasing motivation. Acts of self-control require more effort, inhibition and stress on limited resources [33,34]. When purchasing intention is induced by certain cues, like cuteness, consumers must expend resources to suppress or inhibit unneeded consumption behaviour, such that the behaviour of self-control will spend their resources with the reminders of responsibility [1]. In other words, suppressing the intention for unneeded consumption behaviour would entail further resource loss for consumers [33]. Engaging in uncontrolled acts like unneeded consumption behaviour, therefore, releases consumers from the resource-consuming situation of behavioural inhibition, leading to avoidance of further resource loss (suppressing their buying motivation and causing the loss of energy) and holding onto their current recovery (releasing their stress caused by COVID-19).

Psychological recovery is defined as the period when people return to a normal mode of functioning by removing related stressors [35]. Recovery processes that often occur during vacations can bring relief from negative emotions in life or work [18]. One of the relaxing choices in vacations is purchasing behaviour. Besides satisfying consumers' basic needs, the purchasing process helps them relieve stress by the psychological satisfaction of fulfilling their purchasing impulses. Consumers often can judge whether purchasing behaviour is unneeded after the completion of the consumption process. However, during the purchasing process, it is difficult to recognise redundant shopping because consumers are often immersed in emotional experiences. For example, regarding delicious food, consumers may buy more than they need. When consumers buy more bread than they need, they experience happiness and forget their specific needs at that time.

At the very least, consumers pay attention to the satisfaction derived from purchasing their favourite commodities and neglect whether the quantities they buy outweigh their daily needs. In the short term, consumers tend to focus on psychological needs like hedonic value or positive emotions because they do not have enough time to rationalise their purchasing decision (e.g., whether their purchasing behaviour is overconsumption) [36].

Effecting compliance with their psychological needs can replenish consumers' resources via satisfying basic needs for control [13]. Fritz et al. [37] concluded that there is a beneficial relationship between control perceptions and recovery levels. Additionally, low self-control consumers tend to be motivated to enjoy short-term pleasures, as opposed to high self-control consumers [38]. As a kind of low self-control behaviour, Qin et al. [39] found that abusing others could improve the level of recovery from stressors. In conclusion, the current study suggests that unneeded consumption behaviour might enhance consumers' recovery levels by preventing further resource loss with beneficial self-control and acquiring new resources by improving their sense of relaxation. Thus, we suggest that beneficial control with unneeded consumption behaviour is good for their recovery and propose the following hypothesis:

Hypothesis H1. Engaging in unneeded consumption behaviour is positively related to consumers' own recovery level.

The degree of work engagement fluctuates from one day to another according to individuals' resources differences [18]. For instance, individuals with high work engagement have high levels of energy, dedication and absorption in the workplace [40,41], and high work engagement improves well-being and in-role or extra-role work performance [40,42]. People with high recovery levels are more resilient, even if they face stress and tend to concentrate on their tasks at work and ignore irrelevant cues [18,43]. Therefore, a resource-rich person is full of energy and has enough resources to draw upon, therefore, tends to be more dedicated and concentrate on their task at work. The present study suggests that people with high levels of recovery might enhance employees' work engagement by having enough resources to give them energy and the ability to concentrate on their tasks at work. Previous studies have proved this positive influence of recovery level on work engagement [18,41,44].

Unneeded consumption behaviour also influences work engagement. The current study suggests that the recovery level caused by unneeded consumption behaviour aids consumers' work engagement or investment of physical and psychological energy when they shift enjoyment of consumption to their workplace [43,45]. Unneeded consumption behaviour affects work engagement via recovery level. First, work engagement requires additional personal effort. After unneeded consumption behaviour, sufficient resources are available to concentrate on the task at work. Overconsumption behaviour is very important for consumers to experience positive emotions and employees are willing to expend effort at work [17,46]. Effort expenditure at work can result in strain, whereas during unneeded consumption behaviour, they recover from the previous strain and return to a more relaxed state of feeling refreshed and replenished [47].

Work engagement will benefit from unneeded consumption behaviour. As a result of consumers' unneeded consumption behaviour, individuals wilfully obtain resources needed for high work engagement. Furthermore, recovery levels will also have an impact on work engagement. Additionally, recovery levels play a crucial role in mediating the effect of unneeded consumption behaviour on work engagement. We, therefore, hypothesise the following:

Hypothesis H2. Unneeded consumption behaviour plays an indirect positive role in work engagement through recovery level.

2.1. Personal and Situational Limitations on the Benefits of Unneeded Consumption Behaviour

The mechanism discussed in the above paragraphs—resource recovery—explains how abusive behaviour might aid consumers' work engagement. In the present section, a new question will be discussed from the resource perspective. When unneeded consumption behaviour is beneficial for consumers' engagement in work, COR theory proposes that personal and situational factors constrain people's reactions to the procedures of decreasing net loss and acquiring new resources. Specifically, individual characteristics and environmental factors that engender additional stress after events and reflect these levels of resources are related to resource conservation and gaining processes and might have implications for the resource-related outcomes of unneeded consumption behaviour [29,30]. Importantly, COR theory states that coping events will be beneficial so long as they create no additional stress for actors. However, unneeded consumption behaviour may create additional stress when people perceive the detrimental outcomes to others' well-being, as it violates social environment norms and engenders harm to other people. This additional stress might negate the potential recovery effect from unneeded consumption behaviour.

Additionally, the primacy of loss suggests that the gains of recovery are contingent on whether plentiful resources are available [30,48], and resource acquisitions show greater meaning in situations of scarce resources [48,49]. When consumers find they are in resource-scarce situations (e.g., consumers with high indulgence), the positive impact of unneeded consumption behaviour on recovery can be further strengthened. Accordingly, consumers' perceived consumer effectiveness and indulgence may moderate these recovery processes triggered by unneeded consumption behaviour. In the following section, we explain how these moderators can function in these processes.

Moderating Role of Perceived Consumer Effectiveness

Perceived consumer effectiveness is understood as the idea that self-belief toward individual consumption behaviours can play an effective role in protecting resources [50,51]. Additionally, the level of perceived consumer effectiveness is measured as a judgement of themselves in circumstances from the perspective of the related resources [52,53]. Current studies found that perceived consumer effectiveness is more effective than other indicators, such as environmental concern, green product attitude, or knowledge, to predict environmentally sustainable behaviour [53,54,55], which is important for capturing the desired outcomes of green product purchase [56]. Perceived consumer effectiveness is an environment-oriented motivation that aims to improve the well-being of residents and involves sensitivity to environmental desires.

During the COVID-19 crisis, people tended to conserve the natural environment against more virus infections. In collectivistic cultures [57] such as the Chinese culture, consumers will make purchasing decisions with the motivation of protecting others' health. Unneeded consumption behaviour may damage the environment due to more disposable packages or other harmful materials. In this pandemic, many cities were on mandatory lockdown enforced by the government and necessary goods were very limited. Someone may buy more unneeded products, which may, in turn, be necessary for others. Although unneeded consumption behaviour can aid the recovery process for consumers, such behaviour can also reduce social resources and violate the self-belief of highly perceived consumer effectiveness. Such a violation might cause discomfort or additional stress for consumers as it threatens their good self-image of being a moral representative [58].

While unneeded consumption behaviour has a negative effect on the environment [2], for higher perceived effectiveness consumers, unneeded consumption behaviour violates their ingrained tendency [50], which demonstrates the uncontrolled nature of their behaviour. This decreased sense of control can weaken certain effects of positive emotions, which may be experienced from the enjoyment of unneeded consumption behaviour. However, unneeded consumption behaviour might aid recovery by converting consumers from engaging in resource-consuming situations of self-control to consumers with high-perceived consumer effectiveness, but some additional stress engendered by unneeded consumption behaviour may weaken the gains for recovery [29].

Moreover, high-perceived effective consumers are more likely to protect the environment [56]. Thus, for high-perceived effectiveness consumers, unneeded consumption behaviour tends to violate their ingrained tendency, demonstrating the uncontrolled nature of their behaviour. This decreased sense of control can weaken some recovery effects that may be experienced from the enjoyment of unneeded consumption behaviour. Combining such a relationship with the mediating effect of unneeded consumption behaviour on work engagement through recovery, the present study suggests that perceived consumer effectiveness may attenuate such indirect beneficial effects because recovery tends to lead to gains for resources and enjoying positive emotions in work engagement. Therefore, we propose the following hypothesis:

Hypothesis H3. Perceived consumer effectiveness can moderate the indirect effect of unneeded consumption behaviour on work engagement through recovery level, such that the indirect effect is negatively related to perceived consumer effectiveness.

2.2. Moderating Role of Indulgence

Indulgence captures the extent to which societies allow or promote the gratification related to natural human drives, enjoying life and having fun [59]. The relationship between indulgence and environmental concerns is one of low restraint [60] and it is in this low self-control that unneeded consumption behaviour impacts the recovery level.

Situational characteristics might influence how consumers react to their own unneeded consumption behaviour. Indulgence requires decreased self-control and is often caused by initial resource loss if they are in resource-consuming situations such as incidental damage, life distress or job stress. Consumers tend to indulge and spend when they have made some prepayment of resources, such as money and time [61]. Indulgence is often caused by initial resource loss; consumers will choose indulgence when they confront stress, such as incidental sadness. Thus, consumers high in indulgence experience resource-scarce situations, strengthening the influence of unneeded consumption behaviour on recovery. In particular, unneeded consumption behaviour might improve recovery levels by releasing consumers from such resource-consuming situations of suppressing consumption impulses.

Furthermore, high indulgence demonstrates the opposite situation with regard to self-control. Self-control is required to allocate more resources and energy to balance short and long-term desires [62]. Contrarily, it is easier to consume in high indulgence to satisfy current desires while maintaining sufficient resources because engaging in indulgence can improve consumers' sense of pleasure or happiness [63]. Low self-control consumers would enjoy their consumption experiences when they indulge for no reason [13]. Therefore, there are fewer recovery-based benefits through unneeded consumption behaviour when suppressing indulgence. Consumers can strengthen and repair their mood by indulging in unneeded consumption behaviours and attain more resources for work, based on the recovery level [20]. Hence, we argue that there should be a correlation between indulgence and unneeded consumption behaviour on work engagement. Therefore, the following is proposed:

Hypothesis H4. Indulgence can moderate the positive indirect effect of unneeded consumption behaviour on work engagement through recovery level, such that the direct effect is positively related to indulgence.

...

Conclusion and Implications

Conclusions

The present research introduces a primary trial to discern the benefits of unneeded consumption behaviour to consumers. The shift from consumption to the workplace is especially highlighted with the proximal benefits of unneeded consumption behaviour for actors, including recovery and work engagement. Such beneficial effects can be weakened or strengthened by perceived consumer effectiveness and indulgence, respectively. The findings of short-term benefits (no more than 15 h) can be used to effectively control the frequencies of unneeded consumption behaviour through interventions that help consumers recover at the workplace or change the levels of perceived consumer effectiveness and indulgence. This study may contribute to the trend of exploring how various consumption behaviours influence consumers themselves.

Implications

The current study makes certain theoretical contributions. First, this study broadens the knowledge of unneeded consumption behaviour on the within-personal level. Although previous research has explored various outcomes of unneeded consumption behaviour, the impact of unneeded consumption behaviour on consumers has largely been overlooked. Furthermore, previous studies have focused on the damage or detrimental impacts of overconsumption behaviour, including often cost to consumers and the environment

[72]. However, this study captured the short-term benefits of unneeded consumption behaviour on consumers. To support our hypothesis, we emphasised the finding that unneeded consumption behaviour plays a positive role in work engagement via recovery level.

Second, this study contributes to the consumption theory by illustrating when unneeded consumption behaviour can reveal certain benefits (recovery and work engagement) for consumers. To completely understand the effects of unneeded consumption behaviour on consumers, it is necessary to find the boundary conditions when unneeded consumption behaviour influences actors in weaker or stronger ways. In the perspective of COR, these conditions are revealed both individually (indulgence) and contextually (perceived consumer effectiveness). In particular, unneeded consumption behaviour is beneficial for recovery and engagement at the workplace when consumers have low perceived consumer effectiveness. If consumers have high perceived consumer effectiveness, unneeded consumption behaviour will engender additional resource loss, which weakens the benefits of the recovery and replenishing processes. Meanwhile, the conserving effect of resources also hinges on the extent of indulgence. The benefits of unneeded consumption behaviour on recovery or engagement were stronger when consumers had high indulgence levels.

In practice, these findings may make several contributions. The key findings provide a possible reason why consumers engage in unneeded consumption behaviour. Unneeded consumption behaviour may help consumers conserve their resources by freeing them from resource-consuming situations under which they must control and suppress their impulses. Such resource conservation and gain can shift from consumption to the workplace through work engagement. Unneeded consumption behaviour is not the first order of resource recovery given the harmful effects of unneeded consumption behaviour on the environment. For example, consumers can enjoy tourism as a kind of leisure activity.

The current findings revealed that unneeded consumption behaviour could cause some sense of guilt for consumers with high-perceived consumer effectiveness. These consumers will experience the discomfort of unneeded consumption behaviour when the behaviour harms the environment. Thus, it is easy to control unneeded consumption behaviour by imparting environmental knowledge and emphasising the effectiveness of overconsumption for consumers.

Finally, the current study demonstrated that consumers' perceptions of indulgence could strengthen the relationship between unneeded consumption behaviour and recovery. Another tentative way to control unneeded consumption behaviour is to alleviate consumers' perceptions of high indulgence. For example, consumers experiencing greater consumption happiness can be more satisfied with subsequent indulgence [13]. Some values given to indulgence, such as religiousness, can influence their experiencing happiness [60]. Thus, we can broadcast green values for consumers to reduce their sense of high indulgence and control the occurrences of unneeded consumption behaviour.

...

References

1. Scott M.L., Nenkov G.Y. Using consumer responsibility reminders to reduce cuteness-induced indulgent consumption. Mark. Lett. 2014;27:323–336. doi: 10.1007/s11002-014-9336-8. [DOI] [Google Scholar]
2. Arrow K.J. The Demand for Information and the Distribution of Income. Probab. Eng. Inf. Sci. 1987;1:3–13. doi: 10.1017/S0269964800000243. [DOI] [Google Scholar]
3. Scott C., Johnstone A.M. Stress and Eating Behaviour: Implications for Obesity. Obes. Facts. 2012;5:277–287. doi: 10.1159/000338340. [DOI] [PubMed] [Google Scholar]
4. Kiley M.T. Habit Persistence, Nonseparability between Consumption and Leisure, or Rule-of-Thumb Consumers: Which Accounts for the Predictability of Consumption Growth? Rev. Econ. Stat. 2010;92:679–683. doi: 10.1162/REST_a_00019. [DOI] [Google Scholar]
5. Remko V.H. Research opportunities for a more resilient post-COVID-19 supply chain—Closing the gap between research findings and industry practice. Int. J. Oper. Prod. Manag. 2020;40:341–355. doi: 10.1108/IJOPM-03-2020-0165. [DOI] [Google Scholar]
6. Islam T., Pitafi A.H., Aryaa V., Wang Y., Akhtar N., Mubarik S., Xiaobei L. Panic buying in the COVID-19 pandemic: A multi-country examination. J. Retail. Consum. Serv. 2020;59:102357. doi: 10.1016/j.jretconser.2020.102357. [DOI] [Google Scholar]
7. Taylor S. Understanding and managing pandemic-related panic buying. J. Anxiety Disord. 2021;78:102364. doi: 10.1016/j.janxdis.2021.102364. [DOI] [PubMed] [Google Scholar]

8. Wang H.H., Hao N. Panic buying? Food hoarding during the pandemic period with city lockdown. J. Integr. Agric. 2020;19:2916–2925. doi: 10.1016/S2095-3119(20)63448-7. [DOI] [Google Scholar]
9. Hall C., Fieger P., Prayag G., Dyason D. Panic Buying and Consumption Displacement during COVID-19: Evidence from New Zealand. Economies. 2021;9:46. doi: 10.3390/economies9020046. [DOI] [Google Scholar]
10. Peck J., Shu S.B., editors. Psychological Ownership and Consumer Behavior. Springer Science and Business Media LLC; New York, NY, USA: 2018. pp. 135–144. [Google Scholar]
11. Liu W., Oosterveer P., Spaargaren G. Promoting sustainable consumption in China: A conceptual framework and research review. J. Clean. Prod. 2016;134:13–21. doi: 10.1016/j.jclepro.2015.10.124. [DOI] [Google Scholar]
12. Walla P., Koller M., Meier J.L. Consumer neuroscience to inform consumers—Physiological methods to identify attitude formation related to over-consumption and environmental damage. Front. Hum. Neurosci. 2014;8:304. doi: 10.3389/fnhum.2014.00304. [DOI] [PMC free article] [PubMed] [Google Scholar]
13. Petersen F.E., Dretsch H.J., Loureiro Y.K. Who needs a reason to indulge? Happiness following reason-based indulgent consumption. Int. J. Res. Mark. 2018;35:170–184. doi: 10.1016/j.ijresmar.2017.09.003. [DOI] [Google Scholar]
14. Suzuki S., Hamamura T., Takemura K. Emotional fortification: Indulgent consumption and emotion reappraisal and their implications for well-being. J. Consum. Behav. 2018;18:25–31. doi: 10.1002/cb.1746. [DOI] [Google Scholar]
15. Bahagia B., Nurrahmawati D., Nurhayati I. Resilience of Household Mother in Dealing with Covid-19. Tunas Geogr. 2021;9:129–136. doi: 10.24114/tgeo.v9i2.20843. [DOI] [Google Scholar]
16. Andani K., Wahyono W. Influence of Sales Promotion, Hedonic Shopping Motivation and Fashion Involvement toward Impulse Buying through a Positive Emotion. Manag. Anal. J. 2018;7:448–457. doi: 10.15294/maj.v7i4.24105. [DOI] [Google Scholar]
17. Fredrickson B.L., Levenson R.W. Positive Emotions Speed Recovery from the Cardiovascular Sequelae of Negative Emotions. Cogn. Emot. 1998;12:191–220. doi: 10.1080/026999398379718. [DOI] [PMC free article] [PubMed] [Google Scholar]
18. Sonnentag S. Recovery, work engagement, and proactive behavior: A new look at the interface between nonwork and work. J. Appl. Psychol. 2003;88:518–528. doi: 10.1037/0021-9010.88.3.518. [DOI] [PubMed] [Google Scholar]
19. Guan Y., Deng H., Zhou X. Understanding the impact of the COVID-19 pandemic on career development: Insights from cultural psychology. J. Vocat. Behav. 2020;119:103438. doi: 10.1016/j.jvb.2020.103438. [DOI] [PMC free article] [PubMed] [Google Scholar]
20. Atalay A.S., Meloy M.G. Retail therapy: A strategic effort to improve mood. Psychol. Mark. 2011;28:638–659. doi: 10.1002/mar.20404. [DOI] [Google Scholar]
21. Heppner P.P. Expanding the conceptualization and measurement of applied problem solving and coping: From stages to dimensions to the almost forgotten cultural context. Am. Psychol. 2008;63:805–816. doi: 10.1037/0003-066X.63.8.805. [DOI] [PubMed] [Google Scholar]
22. Hofstede G. Cultures Consequences: International Differences in Work-Related Values. Sage Publications; Beverly Hills, CA, USA: 1980. [Google Scholar]

23. Schwartz S.H., Bilsky W. Toward a universal psychological structure of human values. J. Pers. Soc. Psychol. 1987;53:550–562. doi: 10.1037/0022-3514.53.3.550. [DOI] [Google Scholar]
24. Triandis H.C. Individualism and Collectivism. Routledge; London, UK: 2018. [Google Scholar]
25. Markus H.R., Kitayama S. Culture and the self: Implications for cognition, emotion, and motivation. Psychol. Rev. 1991;98:224–253. doi: 10.1037/0033-295X.98.2.224. [DOI] [Google Scholar]
26. Bulut Z.A., Çımrin F.K., Doğan O. Gender, generation and sustainable consumption: Exploring the behaviour of consumers from Izmir, Turkey. Int. J. Consum. Stud. 2017;41:597–604. doi: 10.1111/ijcs.12371. [DOI] [Google Scholar]
27. Xu J., Schwarz N. Do We Really Need a Reason to Indulge? J. Mark. Res. 2009;46:25–36. doi: 10.1509/jmkr.46.1.25. [DOI] [Google Scholar]
28. Lin S.-H., Ma J., Johnson R.E. When ethical leader behavior breaks bad: How ethical leader behavior can turn abusive via ego depletion and moral licensing. J. Appl. Psychol. 2016;101:815–830. doi: 10.1037/apl0000098. [DOI] [PubMed] [Google Scholar]
29. Hobfoll S.E., Freedy J., Lane C., Geller P. Conservation of Social Resources: Social Support Resource Theory. J. Soc. Pers. Relatsh. 1990;7:465–478. doi: 10.1177/0265407590074004. [DOI] [Google Scholar]
30. Halbesleben J.R.B., Neveu J.-P., Paustian-Underdahl S.C., Westman M. Getting to the "COR". J. Manag. 2014;40:1334–1364. doi: 10.1177/0149206314527130. [DOI] [Google Scholar]
31. Hobfoll S.E. Conservation of resources: A new attempt at conceptualizing stress. Am. Psychol. 1989;44:513–524. doi: 10.1037/0003-066X.44.3.513. [DOI] [PubMed] [Google Scholar]
32. Haws K.L., Bearden W.O., Nenkov G.Y. Consumer spending self-control effectiveness and outcome elaboration prompts. J. Acad. Mark. Sci. 2011;40:695–710. doi: 10.1007/s11747-011-0249-2. [DOI] [Google Scholar]
33. Baumeister R.F., Bratslavsky E., Muraven M., Tice D.M. Ego depletion: Is the active self a limited resource? J. Pers. Soc. Psychol. 1998;74:1252–1265. doi: 10.1037/0022-3514.74.5.1252. [DOI] [PubMed] [Google Scholar]
34. Johnson R.E., Muraven M., Donaldson T.L., Lin S.-H. The Self at Work. Routledge; London, UK: 2017. Self-Control in Work Organizations; pp. 119–144. [Google Scholar]
35. Craig A., Cooper R. State and Trait. Volume 3. Academic Press; London, UK: 1992. Symptoms of Acute and Chronic Fatigue; pp. 289–339. [Google Scholar]
36. Sohn H.-K., Lee T.J. Tourists' impulse buying behavior at duty-free shops: The moderating effects of time pressure and shopping involvement. J. Travel Tour. Mark. 2016;34:341–356. doi: 10.1080/10548408.2016.1170650. [DOI] [Google Scholar]
37. Fritz C., Sonnentag S., Spector P.E., McInroe J.A. The weekend matters: Relationships between stress recovery and affective experiences. J. Organ. Behav. 2010;31:1137–1162. doi: 10.1002/job.672. [DOI] [Google Scholar]
38. Poynor C., Haws K.L. Lines in the Sand: The Role of Motivated Categorization in the Pursuit of Self-Control Goals. J. Consum. Res. 2009;35:772–787. doi: 10.1086/595581. [DOI] [Google Scholar]
39. Qin X., Huang M., Johnson R.E., Hu Q., Ju D. The Short-lived Benefits of Abusive Supervisory Behavior for Actors: An Investigation of Recovery and Work

Engagement. Acad. Manag. J. 2018;61:1951–1975. doi: 10.5465/amj.2016.1325. [DOI] [Google Scholar]

40. Bakker A.B., Schaufeli W., Leiter M., Taris T. Work engagement: An emerging concept in occupational health psychology. Work. Stress. 2008;22:187–200. doi: 10.1080/02678370802393649. [DOI] [PubMed] [Google Scholar]
41. Sonnentag S., Binnewies C., Mojza E.J. Staying well and engaged when demands are high: The role of psychological detachment. J. Appl. Psychol. 2010;95:965–976. doi: 10.1037/a0020032. [DOI] [PubMed] [Google Scholar]
42. Christian M.S., Garza A.S., Slaughter J.E. Work Engagement: A Quantitative Review and Test of Its Relations with Task and Contextual Performance. Pers. Psychol. 2011;64:89–136. doi: 10.1111/j.1744-6570.2010.01203.x. [DOI] [Google Scholar]
43. Kahn W.A. Psychological conditions of personal engagement and disengagement at work. Acad. Manag. J. 1990;33:692–724. doi: 10.2307/256287. [DOI] [Google Scholar]
44. Binnewies C., Sonnentag S., Mojza E.J. Daily performance at work: Feeling recovered in the morning as a predictor of day-level job performance. J. Organ. Behav. 2009;30:67–93. doi: 10.1002/job.541. [DOI] [Google Scholar]
45. Schaufeli W.B., Salanova M., González-Romá V., Bakker A.B. The Measurement of Engagement and Burnout: A Two Sample Confirmatory Factor Analytic Approach. J. Happiness Stud. 2002;3:71–92. doi: 10.1023/A:1015630930326. [DOI] [Google Scholar]
46. Sonnentag S., Mojza E.J., Demerouti E., Bakker A.B. Reciprocal relations between recovery and work engagement: The moderating role of job stressors. J. Appl. Psychol. 2012;97:842–853. doi: 10.1037/a0028292. [DOI] [PubMed] [Google Scholar]
47. Binnewies C., Sonnentag S., Mojza E.J. Feeling recovered and thinking about the good sides of one's work. J. Occup. Health Psychol. 2009;14:243–256. doi: 10.1037/a0014933. [DOI] [PubMed] [Google Scholar]
48. Wells J.D., Hobfoll S.E., Lavin J. Resource Loss, Resource Gain, and Communal Coping During Pregnancy Among Women with Multiple Roles. Psychol. Women Q. 1997;21:645–662. doi: 10.1111/j.1471-6402.1997.tb00136.x. [DOI] [Google Scholar]
49. Vinokur A.D., Schul Y. The web of coping resources and pathways to reemployment following a job loss. J. Occup. Health Psychol. 2002;7:68–83. doi: 10.1037/1076-8998.7.1.68. [DOI] [PubMed] [Google Scholar]
50. Ellen P.S., Wiener J.L., Cobb-Walgren C. The Role of Perceived Consumer Effectiveness in Motivating Environmentally Conscious Behaviors. J. Public Policy Mark. 1991;10:102–117. doi: 10.1177/074391569101000206. [DOI] [Google Scholar]
51. Kinnear T.C., Taylor J.R., Ahmed S.A. Ecologically Concerned Consumers: Who are They? J. Mark. 1974;38:20–24. doi: 10.2307/1250192. [DOI] [Google Scholar]
52. Rejikumar G. Antecedents of Green Purchase Behaviour: An Examination of Moderating Role of Green Wash Fear. Glob. Bus. Rev. 2016;17:332–350. doi: 10.1177/0972150915619812. [DOI] [Google Scholar]
53. Tan B.-C. The Roles of Knowledge, Threat, and PCE on Green Purchase Behaviour. Int. J. Bus. Manag. 2011;6:p14. doi: 10.5539/ijbm.v6n12p14. [DOI] [Google Scholar]
54. Roberts J.A. Green consumers in the 1990s: Profile and implications for advertising. J. Bus. Res. 1996;36:217–231. doi: 10.1016/0148-2963(95)00150-6. [DOI] [Google Scholar]

55. Straughan R.D., Roberts J.A. Environmental segmentation alternatives: A look at green consumer behavior in the new millennium. J. Consum. Mark. 1999;16:558–575. doi: 10.1108/07363769910297506. [DOI] [Google Scholar]
56. Kang J., Liu C., Kim S.-H. Environmentally sustainable textile and apparel consumption: The role of consumer knowledge, perceived consumer effectiveness and perceived personal relevance. Int. J. Consum. Stud. 2013;37:442–452. doi: 10.1111/ijcs.12013. [DOI] [Google Scholar]
57. Hofstede G. Culture's Consequences: Comparing Values, Behaviors, Institutions, and Organizations Across Nations. 2nd ed. Sage Publications; Thousand Oaks, CA, USA: 2001. [Google Scholar]
58. Pepitone A., Festinger L. A Theory of Cognitive Dissonance. Am. J. Psychol. 1959;72:153. doi: 10.2307/1420234. [DOI] [Google Scholar]
59. Cavanaugh L.A. Because I (Don't) Deserve It: How Relationship Reminders and Deservingness Influence Consumer Indulgence. J. Mark. Res. 2014;51:218–232. doi: 10.1509/jmr.12.0133. [DOI] [Google Scholar]
60. Felix R., Hinsch C., Rauschnabel P.A., Schlegelmilch B.B. Religiousness and environmental concern: A multilevel and multi-country analysis of the role of life satisfaction and indulgence. J. Bus. Res. 2018;91:304–312. doi: 10.1016/j.jbusres.2018.06.017. [DOI] [Google Scholar]
61. Besharat A., Nardini G. When indulgence gets the best of you: Unexpected consequences of prepayment. J. Bus. Res. 2018;92:321–328. doi: 10.1016/j.jbusres.2018.07.051. [DOI] [Google Scholar]
62. Laran J. Choosing Your Future: Temporal Distance and the Balance between Self-Control and Indulgence. J. Consum. Res. 2010;36:1002–1015. doi: 10.1086/648380. [DOI] [Google Scholar]
63. Okada E.M. Justification Effects on Consumer Choice of Hedonic and Utilitarian Goods. J. Mark. Res. 2005;42:43–53. doi: 10.1509/jmkr.42.1.43.56889. [DOI] [Google Scholar]
64. Debus M.E., Sonnentag S., Deutsch W., Nussbeck F.W. Making flow happen: The effects of being recovered on work-related flow between and within days. J. Appl. Psychol. 2014;99:713–722. doi: 10.1037/a0035881. [DOI] [PubMed] [Google Scholar]
65. Ilies R., Schwind K.M., Wagner D.T., Johnson M.D., Derue D.S., Ilgen D.R. When can employees have a family life? The effects of daily workload and affect on work-family conflict and social behaviors at home. J. Appl. Psychol. 2007;92:1368–1379. doi: 10.1037/0021-9010.92.5.1368. [DOI] [PubMed] [Google Scholar]
66. Brislin R.W. Back-Translation for Cross-Cultural Research. J. Cross-Cult. Psychol. 1970;1:185–216. doi: 10.1177/135910457000100301. [DOI] [Google Scholar]
67. Lanaj K., Johnson R.E., Barnes C. Beginning the workday yet already depleted? Consequences of late-night smartphone use and sleep. Organ. Behav. Hum. Decis. Process. 2014;124:11–23. doi: 10.1016/j.obhdp.2014.01.001. [DOI] [Google Scholar]
68. Hofmann D.A., Gavin M.B. Centering Decisions in Hierarchical Linear Models: Implications for Research in Organizations. J. Manag. 1998;24:623–641. doi: 10.1177/014920639802400504. [DOI] [Google Scholar]
69. Preacher K.J., Zyphur M.J., Zhang Z. A general multilevel SEM framework for assessing multilevel mediation. Psychol. Methods. 2010;15:209–233. doi: 10.1037/a0020141. [DOI] [PubMed] [Google Scholar]
70. Bauer D.J., Preacher K.J., Gil K.M. Conceptualizing and testing random indirect effects and moderated mediation in multilevel models: New procedures and

recommendations. Psychol. Methods. 2006;11:142–163. doi: 10.1037/1082-989X.11.2.142. [DOI] [PubMed] [Google Scholar]
71. Zhou X., Vohs K.D., Baumeister R.F. The Symbolic Power of Money. Psychol. Sci. 2009;20:700–706. doi: 10.1111/j.1467-9280.2009.02353.x. [DOI] [PubMed] [Google Scholar]
72. Princen T. Consumption and environment: Some conceptual issues. Ecol. Econ. 1999;31:347–363. doi: 10.1016/S0921-8009(99)00039-7. [DOI] [Google Scholar]
73. Podsakoff P.M., MacKenzie S.B., Podsakoff N.P. Sources of Method Bias in Social Science Research and Recommendations on How to Control It. Annu. Rev. Psychol. 2012;63:539–569. doi: 10.1146/annurev-psych-120710-100452. [DOI] [PubMed] [Google Scholar]
74. Edmondson A. Psychological Safety and Learning Behavior in Work Teams. Adm. Sci. Q. 1999;44:350. doi: 10.2307/2666999. [DOI] [Google Scholar]

Viewpoint 4

> "Depression, anxiety, and mental health distress have increased substantially since 2005, when the digital marketplace began to grow."

Humans Are Not Designed for a Consumerist Society

Yuqian Chang and Kristina M. Durante

Humans have only lived a relatively short time in a world where anything we could possibly want is available in stores or at the push of a button. In this paper, Yuqian Chang and Kristina M. Durante argue that our bodies and brains have not changed as fast as the societies we live in, making us unhappy for reasons that are often difficult to articulate. Yuqian Chang is an assistant professor of marketing at Ivey Business School, Western University, and she earned her Ph.D. in Marketing from Rutgers University. Kristina M. Durante is a social psychologist. She is Professor I of marketing, Marketing Department Acting Chair, and the marketing Ph.D. program coordinator at Rutgers Business School.

As you read, consider the following questions:

1. How is modern society different than the way people lived thousands of years ago?
2. According to the authors, in what ways are people suffering in a consumerist society?
3. What possible solutions do the authors give to address these problems?

Abstract

The modern marketplace has made consumers' lives better in many ways, offering a multitude of affordable conveniences and luxuries. Why, then, is the prevalence of physical and mental health deficits higher than any other time in history? Here, we articulate an evolutionary mismatch perspective—the idea that the environment we live in has changed dramatically in a short period of time, but the human body and mind have not changed. Consumers' evolved body and mind are interacting with the modern world as if it was an ancestral environment that existed thousands of years ago, leading to many negative outcomes. We discuss three evolutionary mismatches that contribute to or compound consumer vulnerability to disease and dissatisfaction with life. We review emerging research and propose future directions that inform effective strategies to mitigate illness and enhance wellbeing.

Introduction

The digital marketplace has made consumers' lives better in many ways. Consumers connect to anyone, anywhere in the world in less than a few seconds, order food delivered to doorsteps in minutes, telework from home, and shop online without ever going outside.

Music and television streaming, mobile payment services, and social networking are at the fingertips of most consumers in Western societies. In many ways, consumers are living better than ever before in marketplace history.

Despite these benefits, consumers are less satisfied with life. Americans are the unhappiest they have ever been [1]. Depression, anxiety, and mental health distress have increased substantially since 2005, when the digital marketplace began to grow [2]. The increasing deficits in mental health are particularly evident in young adults. Depression has increased over 50% in adolescents and 63% in people 18e25 years of age since the move to digital [3]. Mood disorder, suicidal ideation, and death by suicide have also increased dramatically since 2005 [4]. Today, suicide is a leading cause of death for people aged 10e35, second only to unintentional injury [5]. The surge in crises of mental health represents a paradox of contemporary consumerism: Given the many conveniences and luxuries accessible to most of the population of our modern world, why are consumers more unhappy than they have ever been? We speculate that the ultimate reason resides within the growing chasm between the environment the human mind and body are designed for and the digital world.

Some proximal outcomes exacerbated by the growing mismatch are documented in literature showing that an abundance of options (i.e., choice overload) can lead to negative outcomes such as decision paralysis, regret, and decreased satisfaction [6,7]. Omnichannel retailing has proliferated the number of product options consumers can seamlessly peruse and, thus, may exacerbate the negative impact of choice on consumer happiness. Consumer materialism has also increased over the past 20 years, particularly in young adults [8]. This may reflect social media's impact on the signal value of consumer products. No longer limited to one's immediate neighborhood, signals can now reach vast numbers of people around the world. Given that materialism is linked to low self-esteem and life satisfaction [9], the recent increase in materialistic values could account for deficits in well-being for modern consumers. Although it is important to understand proximal-level variables that erode consumer wellbeing, an understanding of the ultimate-level source responsible for why consumers are facing rising mental health deficits exposes a multitude of new findings, connections, and blueprints for effective interventions.

Evolutionary mismatch

The precepts of evolutionary mismatch theory are rooted in adaptation by natural selection - the process that shapes behavior and physiology to optimally survive and thrive in an environment. The human mind and body are adapted to survive and thrive in an ancestral environment that existed for 99% of human history. Because the ancestral environment of human brain evolution is very different from our modern environment, an evolutionary mismatch has emerged [10]. People today interact with the Digital Age world using their Stone Age brains designed to confront problems specific to an ancient environment.

This ancient environment was characterized by small group subsistence living, where we were in contact with only about 50e100 people for our entire lives [11]. We lived as hunter-gathers who foraged for food every day to stay alive, often experiencing long periods of fasting [12]. We moved around a lot, often lifting weighted objects. We lived outdoors, having only primitive means for shelter and natural resources for food. Disease, famine, predation, and violent warfare were common threats with little-to-no safeguards. We depended upon those in our small social group for food, shelter, childcare, and protection.

The human brain evolved to solve problems during this period of human existence 300,000 years ago – long before the dawn of agriculture 10,000 years ago, and the industrial revolution a mere 250 years ago, that finally allowed for the mass civilization to (ever slowly) emerge [13]. The process of evolution has not had enough time to change our brains to fit our new world - much less the digital world.

Consumer challenges created by evolutionary mismatch and proposed solutions

Many consumer behaviors are by-products of adaptations that were once beneficial to survival but have since gone awry in our modern world. We discuss three such mismatches below and emerging research relevant to mitigating negative outcomes.

Food

The long-lasting scarcity of nutrients and calories across evolutionary history has led human beings to evolve an innate desire and taste for food essential for survival, namely sugar and fat. While such desire was adaptive for our ancestors to encourage food foraging in past environments, the modern world is populated with caloric abundance. The result is an adaptive proclivity toward high caloric food that is maladapted to current environments. Many of the diseases that exist today result from this mismatch, such as heart disease, obesity, and diabetes [14 - 16]. Poor diet is also related to an increased likelihood of mental illness [17].

Consumer stress, higher today than ever before, makes it more difficult to adhere to a healthy diet [18]. For example, crowding and high population density induce affective thinking, leading to higher caloric intake [19]. Messy living and work spaces inhibit consumers' ability to make healthy food choices [20,21]. Adult consumers who grew up in poor socioeconomic conditions and children in unpredictable, low-income environments eat more even in the absence of hunger [22,23].

Solutions to remedy unhealthy eating are often challenging to execute because adaptations are deeply hardwired into the cognitive architecture of the human mind. Consumers are wired to eat when food is available. Nevertheless, workarounds are possible. Emerging research suggests that social factors, particularly in the digital age, can motivate healthy food choice [24]. Consumers often follow the eating patterns of their romantic partners [25]. Consumers make healthier food choices when motivated to signal status because acts of self-control are associated with high status [26]. Subsequently, reflecting on one's sense of power or control also increases healthy food choices [27]. Rituals such as prayer and mindfulness exercises enacted before food intake facilitate subjective feelings of self-discipline and reduce calorie consumption [29].

Food packaging claims can also encourage healthy food choices [30]. Graphic (versus text) warning labels are more effective in reducing sugary-drink consumption [31]. Highlighting the tastiness of healthy food encourages healthy food choice and satisfaction [32, 33].

Living space

Human beings evolved to live outdoors, with fresh air, natural light, plant life, and variation in temperature. Today, consumers spend more than 90% of their time inside [34]. Living indoors, with exposures to synthetic chemicals and limitations on natural light and vegetation, has made consumers more prone to obesity, infection, allergies, and mental illness [34,35]. This mismatch between the environment the body is designed to live in and modern housing environments, not only makes consumers sick, but it also negatively affects wellbeing and consumer choices [10]. For example, when ambient lighting is dim (vs. bright), consumers' mental alertness is decreased and they are more likely to choose unhealthy food [36].

Innovations in modern housing are working to address these issues of mismatch, particularly those related to overcrowding and air quality [37]. Immediate solutions to encourage better consumer choices involve rematching features within consumer environments to ancestral environments. Natural environments have many cognitive and affective benefits for human beings. For example, office plants help employees recover from visual and mental fatigue [38,39]. Foliage plants at working spaces also enhance workplace satisfaction, concentration, and productivity

[40]. It is also found that plants increase people's creativity [41]. Indoor plants can bring a positive mood [42], as well as feelings of peace and relaxation [43]. Individuals exposed to natural landscapes are more autonomous and generous [44], and put more value on the future versus instant reward [45].

Adding plant images to logos, stores, and business districts enhances consumer attraction and preferences, and perceived service quality [46,47]. Emerging research suggests that staging online real estate with more images containing plants can increase consumers' valuations of the property [48]. Featuring plants in marketing appeals also leads to better persuasion outcomes because plant images increase consumers' perceptions of warmth and trust [49].

Social world

The human mind is designed for social living. Because the quality of our social relationships was critical to survival across human history, most of the emotions we experience are social emotions designed to help us cultivate personal relationships. The social world our brains are designed to respond to is a small one, comprised mostly of extended family [50].

One factor contributing to the recent rise in social anxiety, and crises of mental health more generally, is the disparity between the mass number of individuals in our social world today versus the social world our brain is designed to thrive in. Ancestrally, having trusted family and friends was vital to survival because war, disease, predators, and famine were around every corner. Alliances with others in our group helped us overcome these challenges. Thus, the brain is designed to make us feel unhappy about disappointing people because we used to need these people to secure food, shelter, protection, and mates. Humans are cooperative people pleasers by design. This is especially true for women. Pregnancy, nursing, and childrearingda biological "given" ancestrallydmeant women required even more assistance to keep themselves alive so that children survived [51].

Today, our brains lead us to behave as if the quality of our friendships with other people means the difference between life and death because, for many millennia, it did. Only today, it is impossible to cultivate and tend relationships with all the people we encounter. Social media, television, offices, schools, restaurants, and grocery stores are just some of the venues we see other people every day. At some level, our brain continues to classify all these people as close others we must impress [52e55]. The result is an increased prevalence of social anxiety because our brains are calibrated to the costs associated with social rejection in ancestral environments [56].

Exposure to the multitude of opportunities for perceived social rejection, especially within the digital marketplace, has negatively impacted consumer wellbeing. Research finds that perceptions of others in our social world guide most consumer choices (e.g., food, clothing, music, health care, medicines, exercise, vacations) [57,58]. Social hormones increase consumer attraction to products, particularly those that increase one's social standing (e.g., conspicuous luxury goods) [59 - 61]. The impact of others on consumption is magnified when consumers feel socially rejected or lower in social status compared to others [62]. For example, social rejection leads consumers to spend more money on expensive luxury goods, products that symbolize group membership, and items perceived to be favored by others [63,64]. Increased consumption to compensate for social threats is found to be bidirectional, whereby increased materialism under social threat increases loneliness in consumers, as well as personal debt [65], both of which contribute to mental illness.

Emerging research offers hints at potential workarounds to the negative impact of social relationships on spending. When consumers focus on the intrinsic pleasure their purchases provide, instead of the external value of their possessions, increased loneliness is attenuated [66]. Focusing on the reality that very few others observe our choices also increases consumers' willingness to engage in consumption that benefits the self [67]. The absence of choice and the presence of serendipity improves consumer outcomes. More than just a surprise, serendipity is created through encounters or experiences that are positive, unexpected, and attributed to chance [28]. Removing attribution and deliberation over options leads to greater product enjoyment through the feeling of serendipity (unless the experience has a negative valence; that is, disgust [28]. See Figure 1. Serendipity does not allow for contemplation of the social value of a purchase and, in turn, boosts consumer wellbeing.

Conclusion

The human mind is designed for an ancestral environment that no longer exists, making modern consumers sad and sick. Evolutionary mismatch theory offers a framework to generate predictions about workarounds that can enhance consumer wellbeing. This includes creating contexts today that re-match aspects of ancestral living and reframe the costs and benefits of consumer choices that are suboptimal in the modern marketplace [28,68].

References

Papers of particular interest, published within the period of review, have been highlighted as:

* of special interest

** of outstanding interest

1. Putka S: *Why are Americans getting unhappier, discover*. 2021. https://www.discovermagazine.com/mind/why-are-americansgetting-unhappier.
2. Weinberger AH, Gbedemah M, Martinez AM, Nash D, Galea S, Goodwin RD: **Trends in depression prevalence in the USA from 2005 to 2015: widening disparities in vulnerable groups**. *Psychol Med* 2018, **48**:1308–1315.
3. American Psychological Association: **Mental health issues increased significantly in young adults over last decade**. *Sci Daily* 2019. March 15, https://www.sciencedaily.com/releases/ 2019/03/190315110908.htm; 2019.
4. Twenge JM, Cooper AB, Joiner TE, Duffy ME, Binau SG: **Age, period, and cohort trends in mood disorder indicators and suicide-related outcomes in a nationally representative dataset, 2005-2017**. *J Abnorm Psychol* 2019, **128**:185–199.

5. Centers for Disease Control and Prevention: *Top ten leading causes of death in the U.S. For ages 1-44 from 1981-2020*. National Center for Injury Prevention and Control; 2022. https://www. cdc.gov/injury/wisqars/animated-leading-causes.html. Accessed 8 February 2022.
6. Iyengar SS, Lepper MR: **When choice is demotivating: can one desire too much of a good thing?** *J Pers Soc Psychol* 2000, **79**: 995–1006.
7. Schwartz B: *The paradox of choice: why more is less*. New York: Harper Collins; 2003.
8. Masood A, Musarrat R, Mazahir S: **Increased materialistic trends among youth**. *J Educ Health Commun Psychol* 2017, **5**:56.
9. Marsha LR, Scott D: **A consumer values orientation for materialism and its measurement: scale development and validation**. *J Consum Res* 1992, **19**:303–316.
10. Li NP, van Vugt M, Colarelli SM: **The evolutionary mismatch hypothesis: implications for psychological science**. *Curr Dir Psychol Sci* 2018, **27**:38–44.
11. Dunbar RIM: **Coevolution of neocortical size, group size and language in humans**. *Behav Brain Sci* 1993, **16**:681–735.
12. Rozin P: **Towards a psychology of food and eating: from motivation to module to model to marker, morality, meaning, and metaphor**. *Curr Dir Psychol Sci* 1996, **5**:18–24. 13. Schlebusch CM, Malmström H, Günther T, Sjödin P, Coutinho A, Edlund H, Munters AR, Vicente M, Steyn M, Soodyall H, Lombard M, Jakobsson M: **Southern African ancient genomes estimate modern human divergence to 350,000 to 260,000 years ago**. *Science* 2017, **358**:652–655.
14. Hu FB, Manson JAE, Willett WC: **Types of dietary fat and risk of coronary heart disease: a critical review**. *J Am Coll Nutr* 2001, **20**:5–19.
15. Meyer KA, Kushi LH, Jr DRJ, Slavin J, Sellers TA, Folsom AR: **Carbohydrates, dietary fiber, and incident type 2 diabetes in older women**. *Am J Clin Nutr* 2000, **71**:921–930.
16. Srinivasan K, Viswanad B, Asrat L, Kaul CL, Ramarao P: **Combination of high-fat diet-fed and low-dose streptozotocintreated rat: a model for type 2 diabetes and pharmacological screening**. *Pharmacol Res* 2005, **52**:313–320.
17 * . Marx W, Lane M, Hockey M, Aslam H, Berk M, Walder K, Borsini A, Firth J, Pariante CM, Berding K, Cryan JF, Clarke G, Craig JM, Su KP, Mischoulon D, Gomez-Pinilla F, Foster JA, Cani PD, Thuret S, Staudacher HM, Sánchez-Villegas A, Arshad H, Akbaraly T, O'Neil A, Segasby T, Jacka FN: **Diet and depression: exploring the biological mechanisms of action**. *Mol Psychiatr* 2021, **26**:134–150. This paper provides a comprehensive review of the pathways that modulate how our modern diet of processed foods negatively affects mental health.
18. Vanbergen N, Laran J: **Loss of control and self-regulation: the role of childhood lessons**. *J Consum Res* 2016, **43**:534–548.
19 ** . Hock SJ, Bagchi R: **The impact of crowding on calorie consumption**. *J Consum Res* 2018, **44**:1123–1140. Six studies show that crowding increases calorie intake. This is because crowdedness makes people distracted and decreases cognitive thinking.
20 ** . Chae B, Zhu R: **Environmental disorder leads to selfregulatory failure**. *J Consum Res* 2014, **40**:1203–1218. With four behavioral experiments, this paper shows that environmental disorder (vs. order) increases individuals' perceived lack of control, which leads to regulatory failure in subsequent tasks. For example, disordered environments lead to unhealthy eating and impulse spending. Self-affirmation mitigates this effect.

21. Vohs KD, Redden JP, Rahinel R: **Physical order produces healthy choices, generosity, and conventionality, whereas disorder produces creativity**. *Psychol Sci* 2013, **24**:1860–1867.
22. Proffitt-Leyva RP, Hill SE: **Unpredictability, body awareness, and eating in the absence of hunger: a cognitive schemas approach**. *Health Psychol* 2018, **37**:691–699.
23 ** . Proffitt-Leyva RP, Mengelkoch S, Gassen J, Ellis BJ, Russell EM, Hill SE: **Low socioeconomic status and eating in the absence of hunger in children aged 3–14**. *Appetite* 2020, **154**. Consistent with prior work shown in adults, this paper demonstrates that children growing up in less predictable, less safe environments consume higher amounts of food regardless of current energy needs. This indicates that children in unpredicatable, chaotic environments eat more even when they are not hungry, leading to weight gain.
24 * . Hamilton R, Ferraro R, Haws KL, Mukhopadhyay A: **Traveling with companions: the social customer journey**. J Market 2021, **85**:68–92. This paper formulates the concept of the "social customer journey" and explicates when and how social relationships influence the consumer's path to purchase.
25. Hasford J, Kidwell B, Lopez-Kidwell V: **Happy wife, happy life: food choices in romantic relationships**. *J Consum Res* 2017:1–19.
26. Jones AC, Durante KM, Labroo A: *Conspicuous self-control: when status motives lead consumers to virtue signal.* 2022.
27. Wang CX, Minton EA, Zhang J: **Sense of power: policy insights for encouraging consumers' healthy food choice**. *J Publ Pol Market* 2020, **39**:188–204.
28 ** . Kim A, Affonso FM, Laran J, Durante KM: **Serendipity: chance encounters in the marketplace enhance consumer satisfaction**. *J Market* 2021, **85**:141–157. A series of studies show that serendipity enhances consumer enjoyment. Serendipity is shown to occur when a marketplace encounter is positive, unexpected, and attributed to some degree of chance. This paper demonstrates various ways marketers can create serendipity in product experiences and that choice does not always lead to better outcomes.
29 * . Tian AD, Schroeder J, Häubl G, Risen JL, Norton MI, Gino F: **Enacting rituals to improve self-control**. *J Pers Soc Psychol* 2018, **114**:851–876. Six experiments show that enacting rituals, such as prayer and mindfulness practices, can enhance feelings of self-discipline and self control, leading to healthier food choices and pro-social decision making.
30. André Q, Chandon P, Haws K: **Healthy through presence or absence, nature or science?: a framework for understanding front-of-package food claims**. *J Publ Pol Market* 2019, **38**: 172–191.
31. Donnelly GE, Zatz LY, Svirsky D, John LK: **The effect of graphic warnings on sugary-drink purchasing**. *Psychol Sci* 2018, **29**:1321–1333.
32. Raghunathan R, Naylor RW, Hoyer WD: **The unhealthy = Tasty intuition and its effects on taste inferences, enjoyment, and choice of food products**. *J Market* 2006, **70**:170–184. 33. Finkelstein SR, Fishbach A: When healthy food makes you hungry. *J Consum Res* 2010, 37:357–367.
34. Velux: *Modern indoor living can be bad for your health: new YouGov survey for VELUX sheds light on risks of the "Indoor Generation."* 2018. https://www.prnewswire.com/news-releases/ modern-indoor-living-can-be-bad-for-your-health-new-yougovsurvey-for-velux-sheds-light-on-risks-of-the-indoor-generation300648499.html. Accessed 4 March 2021. 35. Campbell M: *Why do we have allergies?.* OPB; 2018. https://www. opb.org/news/article/why-allergies-summer-pollen-video/.

36 * . Biswas D, Szocs C, Chacko R, Wansink B: **Shining light on atmospherics: how ambient light influences food choices**. *J Market Res* 2017, **54**:111–123. A field study and a series of lab studies show that consumers choose less healthy food options when ambient light luminance is low (vs. high). This is because dim lighting reduces individuals' alertness.

37. World Health Organization: *Housing and health guidelines*. 2018. http://apps.who.int/iris/bitstream/handle/10665/276001/ 9789241550376-eng.pdf.

38. Kondo M, Toriyama T: **Experimental research on the effectiveness of using green in reducing of visual fatigue caused by VDT operation**. *J Jpn Inst Landsc Architect* 1988, **52**:139–144.

39. Shibata S, Suzuki N: **Effects of indoor foliage plants on subjects' recovery from mental fatigue**. *N Am J Psychol* 2001, **3**:385–396.

40. Nieuwenhuis M, Knight C, Postmes T, Haslam SA: **The relative benefits of green versus lean office space: three field experiments**. *J Exp Psychol Appl* 2014, **20**:199–214. 41. Studente S, Seppala N, Sadowska N: **Facilitating creative thinking in the classroom: investigating the effects of plants and the colour green on visual and verbal creativity**. *Think Skills Creativ* 2016, **19**:1–8.

42. Larsen L, Adams J, Deal B, Kweon BS, Tyler E: **Plants in the workplace: the effects of plant density on productivity**. *Attitude Percept Environ Behav* 1998, **30**:261–281.

43. Milligan C, Gatrell A, Bingley A: **"Cultivating health": therapeutic landscapes and older people in northern England**. *Soc Sci Med* 2004, **58**:1781–1793.

44. Weinstein N, Przybylski AK, Ryan RM: *Can nature make us more caring? Effects of immersion in nature on intrinsic aspirations and generosity*. 2009.

45 ** . van der Wal AJ, Schade HM, Krabbendam L, van Vugt M: **Do natural landscapes reduce future discounting in humans?** *Proc Biol Sci* 2013, **280**. Three studies show that exposure to natural rather than urban landscape scenes reduces people's tendency to engage in future discounting. This is because individuals place greater value on the future after exposure to natural scenes.

46. Wolf KL: **Public response to the urban forest in inner-city business districts**. *J Arboric* 2003, **29**:117–126. https://www. researchgate.net/publication/279571942. Accessed 25 April 2021.

47. Brengman M, Willems K, Joye Y: **The impact of in-store greenery on customers**. *Psychol Market* 2012, **29**:807–821.

48. Tifferet S, Vilnai-Yavetz I: **Phytophilia and service atmospherics: the effect of indoor plants on consumers**. *Environ Behav* 2017, **49**:814–844.

49. Chang Y, Ye N, Fong N, Morrin M (Mimi), Huang R: *"Phytophilia premium": assessing the effect of plant images on home buying behavior*. 2022.

50. Chang Y, Durante K, Kim H: *The effect of plants in marketing communications*. 2022. 51. Dunbar RIM: **The anatomy of friendship**. *Trends Cognit Sci* 2018, **22**:32–51.

52. Dufour DL, Sauther ML: **Comparative and evolutionary dimensions of the energetics of human pregnancy and lactation**. *Am J Hum Biol* 2002, **14**:584–602. 53. Barkow JH: Darwin, sex, and status: biological approaches to mind and culture. Toronto, ON: University of Toronto Press; 1989.

54. Barkow JH: **Beneath new culture is old psychology: gossip and social stratification**. In *The adapted mind: evolutionary psychology and the generation of culture*. Edited by Barkow JH, Tooby J, Cosmides L, Oxford, UK: Oxford University Press; 1992: 627–637.

55. De Backer CJS, Nelissen M, Vyncke P, Braeckman J, McAndrew FT: **Celebrities: from teachers to friends**. *Hum Nat* 2007, **18**:334–354.

56. Kanazawa S: **Bowling with our imaginary friends**. *Evol Hum Behav* 2002, **23**:167–171. 57. Maner JK, Kenrick DT: **When adaptations go awry: functional and dysfunctional aspects of social anxiety**. *Social Iss Pol Rev* 2010, **4**:111–142.
58. Bellezza S, Francesca G, Anat K: **The red sneakers effect: inferring status and competence from signals of nonconformity**. *J Consum Res* 2017, **41**:35–54.
59. McFerran B, Dahl DW, Fitzsimons GJ, Morales AC: **I'll have what she's having: effects of social influence and body type on the food choices of others**. *J Consum Res* 2010, **36**: 915–926.
60. Durante KM, Griskevicius V, Hill SE, Perilloux C, Li NP: **Ovulation, female competition, and product choice: hormonal influences on consumer behavior**. *J Consum Res* 2011, **37**: 921–934.
61. Durante KM, Griskevicius V, Cantú SM, Simpson JA: **Money, status, and the ovulatory cycle**. *J Market Res* 2014, **51**:27–39.
62. Nave G, Nadler A, Zava D, Camerer C: **Single-Dose testosterone administration impairs cognitive reflection in men**. *Psychol Sci* 2017, **28**:1398–1407.
63. Mandel N, Rucker DD, Levav J, Galinsky AD: **The compensatory consumer behavior model: how self-discrepancies drive consumer behavior**. *J Consum Psychol* 2017, **27**:133–146.
64. Lee J, Shrum LJ: **Conspicuous consumption versus charitable behavior in response to social exclusion: a differential needs explanation**. *J Consum Res* 2012, **39**:530–544.
65. Mead NL, Maner JK: **On keeping your enemies close: powerful leaders seek proximity to ingroup power threats**. *J Pers Soc Psychol* 2012, **102**:576–591.
66. Pieters R: **Bidirectional dynamics of materialism and loneliness: not just a vicious cycle**. *J Consum Res* 2013, **40**:615–631.
67. Ratner RK, Hamilton RW: **Inhibited from bowling alone**. *J Consum Res* 2015, **42**:266–283.
68 ** . Ross GR, Meloy MG, Bolton LE: **Disorder and downsizing**. *J Consum Res* 2021, **47**:959–977. Nine studies show that disordered setup reduces within-category comparison and encourages consumers to engage in downsizing. This effect is moderated by consumers' comparison tendencies, waste aversion, and decision strategy (selection vs. rejection).

Periodical and Internet Sources Bibliography

The following articles have been selected to supplement the diverse views presented in this chapter.

Mai Dao, La-Bhus Fah Jirasavetakul, and Jing Zhou, "Drivers of Post-COVID Private Consumption in the U.S.," IMF e-Library, June 21, 2024. www.elibrary.imf.org/view/journals/001/2024/128/article-A001-en.xml.

"Does Consuming Make You Happier?," Monash University, October 28, 2015. impact.monash.edu/economy/does-consuming-make-you-happier.

Adam Hayes, "Consumerism: Definition, Economic Impact, Pros & Cons," Investopedia, July 14, 2024. www.investopedia.com/terms/c/consumerism.asp.

Enisse Kharroubi and Emanuel Kohlscheen, "Consumption-Led Expansions," March 2017. www.bis.org/publ/qtrpdf/r_qt1703e.pdf.

"Positives of Consumerism," History Crunch. www.historycrunch.com/consumerism-positives.html.

Alexander Richter and Xioaqing Zhou, "Strength in Consumer Spending Does Not Necessarily Imply Low Probability of Recession," Federal Reserve Bank of Dallas, January 2, 2024. www.dallasfed.org/research/economics/2024/0102.

Brian Roach, Neva Goodwin, and Julie Nelson, "Consumption and the Consumer Society," Global Development And Environment Institute at Tufts University, 2019. https://www.bu.edu/eci/files/2019/10/Consumption_and_Consumer_Society.pdf.

Leslie Woolums, "The Excessive Nature of Overconsumption in American Culture," University of Alabama at Birmingham Institute for Human Rights Blog, October 24, 2023. sites.uab.edu/humanrights/2023/10/24/the-excessive-nature-of-overconsumption-in-american-culture/.

CHAPTER 2:

Who Is Most Responsible for Overconsumption?

Chapter Preface

Overconsumption is a growing global concern, linked to environmental destruction, resource depletion, and rising levels of waste. But when it comes to assigning responsibility, the answers are far from simple. Is it the fault of individuals who buy more than they need? Do corporations, advertisers, and governments play a larger role by encouraging unsustainable habits and prioritizing profit over the planet?

This chapter explores the debate over who bears the greatest responsibility for overconsumption. Some contributors argue that personal choices matter most—consumers have the power to say no, buy less, and live more sustainably. Others point to systemic forces: marketing strategies that promote constant upgrades, industries that depend on planned obsolescence, and policies that favor economic growth over environmental protection.

Questions of class, culture, and global inequality also emerge. The lowest-income Americans and Europeans are still wealthier than the lowest-income individuals in less wealthy countries. What is the cutoff point when we talk about "the rich"? Is it logical or is it classist to suggest that low-income individuals in wealthy countries should make changes to their consumption patterns?

By examining the roots of overconsumption from multiple perspectives, this chapter encourages readers to think critically about accountability, power, and the possibility of real change.

Viewpoint 1

> *"Although consumption has steadily increased around the world, it would be unfair to suggest that everybody—or every country—is equally responsible for pulling humanity across the threshold into unsustainability."*

People in Wealthy Countries Consume More

Seth Millstein

The rise in availability of relatively cheap items has also given rise to thoughtless consumerism and overconsumption. The mindset of "I might not end up needing it, but it's only $10" gives those with enough money a mental permission slip to overconsume. Discarding the unused items causes more environmental problems. In this viewpoint, Seth Millstein points out that this type of thoughtless overconsumption is primarily driven by people in wealthy countries. Seth Millstein is a writer who lives in the Bay Area.

As you read, consider the following questions:

1. Why is overconsumption so bad for the environment?
2. How can we mitigate the problems of overconsumption, such as the food waste inherent in our supply chain?
3. What can you as an individual do to curb overconsumption?

"How Overconsumption Affects the Environment and Health, Explained" by Seth Millstein, Sentient Media, January 4, 2024. Reprinted by permission.

Of all the human practices that are gradually destroying the environment, overconsumption is one of the most significant and least discussed. We are using up our planet's resources faster than they can regenerate, and a look at how overconsumption affects the environment and global health makes it abundantly clear that if we want to continue living on planet Earth, we need to make some serious changes, and fast.

Overconsumption is when humans consume more resources than we produce. At the smallest scale, this occurs at the individual level, but overconsumption is more commonly measured on a country-wide, continent-wide or planet-wide basis.

"We live on a finite planet that cannot support endless growth and unequitable, unchecked consumption," Jennifer Molidor, Senior Food Campaigner at the Center for Biological Diversity, told Sentient via email. "The pressure to constantly consume is driving destructive resource extraction, pollution and waste, and contributing to the climate and extinction crises."

No matter how you look at it, the upshot is the same: If we use resources at a faster rate than we can regrow or extract them, we'll eventually run out of resources. And unfortunately, that's exactly what we're doing.

Is Overconsumption Getting Worse?

Consumption rates differ wildly from region to region, but on a global basis, they've been steadily increasing over the decades. One way of seeing this is by looking at what's called Earth Overshoot Day, a metric devised by Global Footprint Network to measure consumption over time.

Every year has an overshoot day. It's the date on which humanity's consumption of resources exceeded the planet's ability to regenerate those resources within the year. The mere fact that there is an Earth overshoot day is good evidence of our overconsumption, but what's equally concerning is that overshoot day has been coming earlier and earlier by the year.

In 1972, for instance, overshoot day fell on December 27; this means that in 1972, we were almost "living within our means," from a global resources standpoint. In 2024, however, overshoot day fell on August 1.

To put it differently: In 1972, we would have needed 1.01 Earths to support our consumption habits, but by 2024, we'd need 1.7 Earths to provide enough resources to match our consumption.

Some of this increase is attributable to population growth, as the total number of humans on Earth has more than doubled since the early 1970s. But that can't be the only explanation, because worldwide resource extraction quadrupled over that same period of time, according to an unpublished United Nations report reviewed by the Guardian. This shows that consumption has been rising on a per capita basis, as well as an absolute one, over time.

How Food Waste Contributes to Overconsumption

Over the last half-century, meat consumption in particular has risen dramatically. In 1961, the average person ate around 51 pounds of meat per year; by 2021, they were consuming 94 pounds of meat per year. Perhaps the most frustrating element of the consumption equation, though, is the astonishing amount of food that is created but not eaten. A staggering one-third of all food on the planet is wasted every year, and around one-fourth of all animals killed for food are never actually eaten. Some of this is due to businesses and individuals throwing away leftovers, but a much bigger share of food — almost 50 percent — is lost during the production process itself.

"Food waste is part and parcel of our overconsumption," Molidor says. "And this happens in the food chain at every level, from farm to fork, from supermarkets and restaurants to households."

Whether it's crop pests, livestock diseases or animals dying in transit, our current system of food production results in around 1.3 billion tons of wasted food annually, which is also an enormous contributor to overconsumption.

What Drives Overconsumption?

All of this raises the question: What causes overconsumption, and why has it been getting worse over time?

"First and foremost, it's our economic model," Laura Fox, environmental lawyer and research scholar at Yale Law School, tells Sentient. "Capitalism promotes constant growth and rewards consumerism, and that mindset leads to overconsumption, and people buying more than what they need."

The recent worsening of overconsumption is largely the result of technological advances, which have caused significant changes on both the supply and the demand side of the equation.

From a supply standpoint, technological advances have increased production capacity, making it cheaper than ever to pump out as much product as possible. From a demand standpoint, new technology has resulted in people seeing exponentially more advertisements than they used to, and enabled advertisers to more effectively reach their target audiences.

Last but not least, online shopping has dramatically expanded our access to goods and services, making it easier for people to buy whatever's being advertised.

"It's very easy to just go on a particular online marketplace and have any goods delivered to your home, sometimes within the same day," Fox tells Sentient. "And having that ease, and products available more cheaply than they might have been otherwise, can help contribute to this pattern of consuming more than is necessary."

Who's Most Responsible for Overconsumption

Although consumption has steadily increased around the world, it would be unfair to suggest that everybody—or every country—is equally responsible for pulling humanity across the threshold into unsustainability.

Higher-income countries consume six times more resources than low-income countries, according to a UNEP report. In North America, the average person consumes nine times as many natural resources as the average person in Africa.

The Consequences of Overconsumption

Many researchers and organizations have attempted to predict the long-term future impacts of overconsumption, and the predictions are pretty grim. The Organisation For Economic Cooperation and Development predicts that by 2050, PM (particulate matter) polluted air will kill three times as many people as it had in 2000. Plastic in the ocean is expected to quadruple over that same period, according to the WWF, while the Millennium Alliance for Humanity and Biosphere warns that global oil reserves could be entirely depleted by 2052.

It makes sense that much of the discussion about overconsumption focuses on long-term projections; if we continue to use our planet's resources faster than they can be generated, we'll eventually run out of resources, which would quite literally threaten humanity's existence.

That said, some of overconsumption's consequences are already observable. The staggering amount of plastic in the ocean is a prime example of this: Around 6.6 million tons of plastic waste ends up in waterways every year, wreaking havoc on coastal communities and producing trash islands like the Great Pacific Garbage Patch.

Overconsumption's Impact on the Environment and Health

Overconsumption is inextricably linked to natural resource extraction. Brazilian rainforests are razed to produce lumber, or to clear the way for mining and agricultural development. Copper is used to make everything from kitchen sinks and jewelry to electrical wires and cell phones. And of course, oil is mined to fuel the many vehicles humans use to travel the world.

One stark example of how the over-extraction of resources affects the environment and health is the Niger Delta. The Niger Delta is one of the world's largest wetlands, and was once a rich and fertile ecosystem with thriving farmlands and fisheries. However, nearly a century of oil extraction has wrought havoc on the region's ecosystem and inhabitants. Thanks to the harmful chemicals that are released into the air during the oil extraction process, it now rains acid in the Niger Delta, which corrodes roofs and building structures, destroys crops and pollutes water sources across the delta.

But the human toll of this resource extraction is even more horrifying. Many residents of the delta suffer from breathing problems and chronic bronchitis, and a 2021 study found that cancer rates are much higher in the delta than in non-oil-producing parts of Nigeria. Tragically, as a result of these and other adverse health effects of oil extraction, the life expectancy in the Niger Delta is around 40 years.

In Brazil, almost 20 percent of the entire Amazon has been deforested, according to the Council For Foreign Relations, largely for logging and cattle farming. As a result of this widespread destruction, there has been mass soil erosion, loss of biodiversity and increased CO2 emissions in the Amazon. Deforestation has also killed scores of animals who live in the Amazon and endangered the livelihoods of local Indigenous people.

Overfishing and Its Impact on Overconsumption

Meanwhile, oceans around the world have been overfished to produce seafood, which poses a serious threat to fish populations. Overfishing occurs when people catch fish and other sea creatures at a higher rate than they can reproduce. The practice has put over one-third of all sharks, rays and chimeras at risk of going extinct, according to the WWF, and around one-third of all fisheries are now at risk of depopulation thanks to overfishing, according to the Sierra Club.

Overfishing is also costing people jobs: When Canada's Grand Banks cod fishery collapsed in 1992 due to overfishing, over 35,000 people who worked in the local seafood industry were put out of work.

Given how widespread overfishing is, it's no surprise that the seafood industry is also one of the biggest offenders when it comes to food waste. As previously mentioned, around a quarter of all animals farmed for food are never eaten — but in the U.S., that number rises to almost 50 percent when it comes to seafood.

All of this resource extraction can be linked back to overconsumption. Oceans are overfished to feed global demand for seafood, which is expected to double by 2050.

It's also worth noting that an estimated 75 percent of the plastic waste in the Great Pacific Garbage Patch comes from fishing gear—yet another way in which overconsumption leads to more plastic in the planet's oceans.

How to Fight Overconsumption

So, how can we go about reversing these trends? At the individual level, the answer is obvious: by consuming less. But how do we do that?

Limiting Overconsumption on the Individual Level

There are plenty of practical steps individuals can take to reduce their consumption. Using reusable containers and products as opposed to disposable ones is a great place to start. Switching to paperless billing, buying food in glass containers instead of plastic ones, and using a hybrid or electric vehicle are also good opportunities to use fewer natural resources in your day-to-day life.

Another way of fighting overconsumption is to reduce your meat and dairy consumption. Meat production is terrible for the planet, and those of us in the global north already eat much more meat than we need to. Adopting a plant-based diet is an excellent way to bring your individual consumption down to more sustainable levels, Fox says.

"Purchasing more plant-based products is more efficient, because you're directly consuming those calories," Fox tells Sentient, "versus having the calories being processed through animal products to then be converted into calories for human consumption."

However, some activists have argued that the best way for individuals to consume fewer resources is to simply to spend less money across the board, regardless of what that money is spent on.

JB MacKinnon, a Canadian journalist and author of the book "The Day The World Stopped Shopping," is one such person. He has written and spoken at length about the dangers of overconsumption, and argues that the adoption of green technology—well-intentioned as it may be—is ultimately less effective in protecting the environment than reducing consumption of all products, green or not, across the board.

"If you want a rule of thumb for how much impact you're having as a consumer, the best one is: how much money are you spending?," MacKinnon told the *Guardian*. "If it's increasing, you're probably increasing your impact; if it's lowering, you're probably lowering your impact."

How to Combat Overconsumption on a Global Scale

The onus for fighting overconsumption shouldn't fall only on consumers, as governments have a number of tools at their disposal for doing so as well.

One such tool is legislation. Governments can incentivize people and businesses to adopt sustainable energy systems, like solar power, by offering tax credits or subsidies to those who do. They can also establish certification programs for environmentally friendly products, provide support and services to businesses that want to implement greener practices and launch public education campaigns addressing overconsumption. In addition, localities can adjust their own procurement policies to prioritize more environmentally efficient foods, Fox says, a step several cities and counties around the U.S. have already taken. In practice, this means "purchasing fewer high-emissions and high-impacts foods, like meat and dairy," Molidor adds. Similarly, schools that serve lunch to their students can implement policies to reduce food waste, and incorporate more plant-based foods into their menus.

In theory, corporations could take steps to reduce overconsumption as well. In practice, they usually don't, because they profit from it: in a capitalist system, "consuming" usually entails purchasing a good, and selling goods is how businesses make money.

"There's not a lot of huge incentives for companies to stop producing and getting people to buy their products," Fox says. "[Overconsumption] is such a systemic problem, and it's perpetuated by large corporations whose interest lay in the consumption of their goods and services."

The Bottom Line

Overconsumption is a tricky issue to conceptualize because on a basic level, we all need to consume to survive. It's also not fair to solely blame individuals for this problem, as modern society is structured in a way that encourages overconsumption.

But the wide-reaching environmental and global health consequences of our current practices make it abundantly clear that we're consuming a lot more than we need to. Unless we make a change, overconsumption will destroy our ecosystems—and possibly humanity's ability to live within them.

Viewpoint 2

> *"From the 2008 financial crisis, to the pandemic and the increasingly severe impacts of climate change—disruptive events tend to hit the poorest first and hardest."*

The Rich Are Most Responsible for Overconsumption

Laura Paddison

In American society, people are bombarded with messages urging them to consume. Corporations put advertisements everywhere, the government champions spending as a way to support the country's economy, and influencers on social media show off rooms full of items. The more money a person has, the more they can—and typically do—spend on unnecessary items and experiences. In this viewpoint, Laura Paddison suggests that the world's richest people are the ones who are most responsible for overconsumption, simply because they are the ones who have the means to buy the most. Paddison is a writer who focuses mainly on climate issues.

As you read, consider the following questions:

1. How are the actions of the rich affecting the world's poor?
2. According to the viewpoint, is your family part of the world's richest 10 percent?

"How the rich are driving climate change" by Laura Paddison, BBC, 28 October 2021. Reprinted by permission.

3. How are individual and systemic actions intertwined?

In 2018, Stefan Gössling and his team spent months scouring the social media profiles of some of the richest celebrities, from Paris Hilton to Oprah Winfrey. The tourism professor from Linnaeus University in Sweden was looking for evidence of how much they were flying.

The answer was a lot. Bill Gates, one of the world's most high-profile environmental advocates, took 59 flights in 2017, according to Gössling's calculations, covering a distance of around 343,500km (213,000 miles) – more than eight times around the world – generating more than 1,600 tonnes of greenhouse gases (that's equivalent to the average yearly emissions of 105 Americans).

Gössling's aim was to try to uncover the individual consumption levels of the mega rich, whose lifestyles are often shrouded in secrecy. His research coincided with a growing environmental movement, spearheaded by Greta Thunberg, which put a spotlight on personal accountability. Flying, one of the most carbon-intensive forms of consumption, became a symbol of this new accountability.

"The bigger your carbon footprint, the bigger your moral duty," Thunberg wrote in the *Guardian* in 2019.

The last few decades have shone a spotlight on global inequality. From the 2008 financial crisis, to the pandemic and the increasingly severe impacts of climate change – disruptive events tend to hit the poorest first and hardest.

But in debates about how to solve inequality, overconsumption is often overlooked. "Each unit you overshoot means someone has to give [something] up," says Lewis Akenji, managing director of Hot or Cool Institute, a Berlin-based think tank. As a result, the outsized carbon footprints of society's richest entrench inequality and threaten the world's ability to stave off catastrophic climate change.

The statistics are startling. The world's wealthiest 10% were responsible for around half of global emissions in 2015, according to a 2020 report from Oxfam and the Stockholm Environment Institute. The top 1% were responsible for 15% of emissions, nearly twice as much as the world's poorest 50%, who were responsible for just 7% and will feel the brunt of climate impacts despite bearing the least responsibility for causing them.

As the rich race through the remaining "carbon budget" – the amount of greenhouse gas it's possible to emit without pushing the world beyond 1.5C of warming by the end of the century – they "aren't making the space for the bottom 50% of the population to grow their emissions to the point where they're actually getting their needs met", says Emily Ghosh, a staff scientist at the Stockholm Environment Institute.

Dario Kenner, the author of *Carbon Inequality: The Role of the Richest in Climate Change*, coined the term "polluter elite" to describe the wealthiest in society who invest extensively in fossil fuels, as well as having a strong climate impact from their high-carbon lifestyles. But while the polluter elite have a disproportionate impact, the world's wealthiest encompasses a much broader swathe of the population (see fact box below).

Who is the 1%?

When we think of "the rich", we might think of millionaires and billionaires with private jets and multiple mansions.

But an income of $38,000 (£27,500) is enough to put someone in the world's richest 10%, and $109,000 (£79,000) puts them in the top 1%.

Oxfam/Stockholm Environment Institute

As things stand, most people in wealthy countries are consuming in ways that are accelerating climate catastrophe. When you take into account the emissions from imported goods, the average person in the UK emits 8.5 tonnes of carbon a year according to the Hot or Cool Institute, a figure that rises to 14.2 tonnes in Canada, the country with highest emissions among those the institute surveyed. In order to stay within 1.5C of warming, these figures need to come down dramatically to 0.7 tonnes per person by 2050.

Personal consumption is a thorny topic to address. It can quickly spiral into a well-worn debate about whether tackling climate change hinges on individual actions or systemic changes from governments and corporations.

"This is a false dichotomy," says Akenji. "Lifestyles don't exist in a vacuum, lifestyles are shaped by context." People live their lives within the mostly unsustainable political and economic systems that exist. But, without addressing the lifestyles of the wealthiest and most polluting in our societies, and the power they hold, we won't be able to address climate change.

"Wealthy people set the tone on consumption to which everybody aspires. That's where the toxic effects are," says Halina Szejnwald Brown, professor emerita of environmental science and policy at Clark University in the US.

Take aviation. "As soon as you fly, you belong to a global elite," says Gössling. More than 90% of people have never flown and just 1% of the world's population is responsible for 50% of emissions from flying. From the business elite crisscrossing the globe to the celebrities who have made travel part of their personal brands, their behaviour has helped make a high carbon lifestyle aspirational and desirable, says Gössling.

The SUVs that ferry around presidents, business leaders and celebrities – and increasingly middle class families in cities – have also become a status symbol despite their environmental impact. Making up 42% of global car sales in 2019, SUVs were the only sector to see emissions rise in 2020. The increase in people buying SUVs last year effectively cancelled out the climate gains of electric cars.

Bigger homes are another consumption hotspot. "Housing choices signify prestige and social status," writes Kimberly Nicholas, a sustainability scientist at Lund University, and her co-authors in a recent study on the role of wealthy people in driving climate change. In Europe, nearly 11% of emissions from housing came from the top 1% of emitters who own large—and often multiple—homes.

The last few years, however, have seen social norms start to shift. In Sweden, Thunberg's activism helped inspire flygskam (the Swedish word for "flight shame"), a concept which led people to question how much they should be flying. The movement was linked to a 4% drop in the number of people flying from Sweden's airports in 2018 – a rare fall at a time when global passenger numbers were increasing.

Covid-19, which dramatically curtailed business travel, proved that video calls can replace in-person meetings. A Bloomberg survey found 84% of businesses plan to spend less on work travel post-pandemic.

People have also started to consider the impact of their diets, leading to a boom in plant-based meat and dairy companies. "That's not coming from an edict or a government policy requirement," says Peter Newell, a professor of international relations at the University of Sussex. "That's just businesses seeing that's where the market is shifting."

But these changes are too gradual for the emergency we are in, says Kenner: "We're going past climate tipping points and species are going extinct." The issue is about speed, and for that government action is necessary, he says.

Targeted taxes on unsustainable behaviours, such as frequent flying and the overconsumption of meat, could help shift people to low carbon behaviours more quickly, says Newell, especially if there is a direct link between punishing polluting behaviour and investments that benefit many.

For example, proceeds from a frequent flyer tax could be invested into a cheaper or even free public transport system, and money from a "mansion tax" could be put towards insulating houses, bringing down levels of fuel poverty. The problem, though, is if the richest can simply absorb these costs and continue as before.

A more radical idea is a personal carbon allowance (PCA), where individuals are allocated an equal, tradable carbon allowance. If people want to emit more, they must buy the unwanted allowances of others. Versions of a PCA have been explored in Ireland, France, and California. In 2018, the UK government analysed its feasibility but concluded that a PCA would be too expensive, difficult to administer and unlikely to be accepted socially.

But in the context of a climate emergency and a pandemic, which has forced people to accept individual restrictions in the name of collective gain, it may be a policy worth reconsidering, according to a recent analysis.

A PCA is appealing on one level, says Newell, "because it makes it really clear what our per capita entitlements are." But, he adds, "it's an extreme version of individualising responsibility." It could end up unjustly penalising people who, for example, live in areas with few public transport options.

Another policy idea that's gaining popularity is "choice editing", where governments restrict carbon-intensive products – like private jets or mega yachts – from coming to market in the first place. The idea is low-carbon options, many of which already exist, will fill the gap.

Choice editing may sound radical but it's not new, says Akenji. The UK government, for example, uses choice editing on public safety grounds to ban the sale of guns or cars with no seatbelts. "Undoing unsustainable behaviours is a whole lot harder than preventing unsustainable products from coming to market in the first place," concluded an April report on behaviour change co-authored by Newell.

But even as time runs out for tackling climate change, many governments baulk at behaviour-change policies fearing they will be politically toxic to voters and unpalatable to the rich. The control that the wealthiest have over governments through lobbying and hefty donations gives them huge influence to dilute climate action and shape the choices available for everyone, says Kenner. "There's this other future, this alternative future, which is being denied on a daily basis," he says.

For all the policies that target the behaviour of consumers, ultimately, it's very hard to bring down emissions if the infrastructure isn't there for people to live low-carbon lives. "There's a lot that needs to go into building a more sustainable society and it's beyond just reducing private jets and luxury yachts," says Ghosh.

Some governments are making big changes. The Welsh government has suspended investment in new road building to meet emissions targets, the Netherlands has proposed cutting livestock numbers by 30% to reduce pollution and councils in UK cities such as Norwich and Exeter have started building energy-efficient social housing.

Others have targeted the role of advertising in driving unsustainable consumption. "People try to stake out their place in society by distinguishing themselves from those that are below them," says Brown, and advertising "builds its entire industry on this insecurity." In 2021, Amsterdam banned adverts for emissions-intensive products including SUVs and cheap short-haul flights, following in the footsteps of cities such as São Paulo and Chennai, which have banned or strictly limited billboard advertising.

"But this is really not enough," says Akenji. The pace is glacial and the world is running out of time. Governments need to overhaul infrastructure, he says, putting sustainability at the heart of policy. That means creating fast, extensive and affordable public transport networks; decarbonising electricity; building denser, well-insulated housing; banning the use of gas-powered cars; and considering measures such as a four-day working week.

Governments and the wealthy, with their outsized role in influencing social norms, can also help to change the narrative that climate action is all about loss of personal freedom and quality of life. "The sad thing about this is that things that have been shown to be more sustainable for the environment are almost always better for our own wellbeing and social cohesion," says Akenji.

Eating less meat has health benefits. Having fewer SUVs and gas-powered cars increases the air quality and reduces air pollution deaths. And a four-day working week could allow for a better work life balance, more family time and fewer child-care costs for parents.

"No one gets up in the morning and says, 'I'm going to wreck the environment,'" says Akenji. People consume for many reasons: to meet their needs, to show affection, to feel good or because they feel pressured into it by advertising or social expectations.

Very few people ever really question their consumption, says Brown. "These are pretty deep questions: 'Who am I and what do I need for a good life?' I mean, how many people want to sit down and actually ask that question?"

Individual actions won't be enough to tackle climate change, says Akenji, and guilt and shame won't help. But choices and actions do matter. "I think we should all become political activists in one way or another," he says. "What we're going to do is very deliberately and decisively go after our governments and ask them to live up to their commitments."

Viewpoint 3

> *"By educating people about family planning, contraception, population growth factors and trends, and other relevant topics, we can empower individuals to make informed decisions about their reproductive health."*

Overpopulation Is Driving Consumption

Natalia Kolkowska

People have basic needs to meet. The more people there are in the world, the more resources will be used, even before accounting for individual overconsumption. In this viewpoint, Natalia Kolkowska states that better access to contraceptives and family planning education are two ways we can help people reduce the number of children they have, thereby gradually lessening overpopulation. Kolkowska is a linguist and writer who is passionate about the topic of sustainability.

As you read, consider the following questions:

1. How does overpopulation affect people and the planet?
2. What are the benefits of family planning education?
3. Why are contraception and family planning not enough of a solution on their own?

"How Does Overpopulation Affect Sustainability? Challenges and Solutions" by Natalia Kolkowska, Earth.Org, May 15, 2023. Reprinted by permission.

The world's population has been growing exponentially over the past decades, from around 2 billion in 1900 to more than 8 billion now, and is expected to continue growing in the coming decades. While the increase in the number of people can be seen as a positive development, it also poses a significant challenge to sustainability. In this article, we try to answer the following questions: How does overpopulation affect sustainability and what challenges does this trend pose? What are the potential solutions to address these challenges and create a more sustainable future for all?

By educating people about family planning, contraception, population growth factors and trends, and other relevant topics, we can empower individuals to make informed decisions about their reproductive health. The world's increasing population is directly impacting sustainability, as more people require resources to survive. Below, we examine the various issues that arise from overpopulation and their effects on sustainability.

Climate Change

Increasing population levels lead to increased consumption of resources, resulting in greater greenhouse gas emissions. This contributes to climate change and can have a devastating effect on the environment.

Resource Depletion

More people require more food, water, energy, and other resources for their own survival. As these become increasingly scarce due to overpopulation, it becomes harder for us to sustain our current way of life.

Environmental Degradation

As more people consume resources, they create waste and pollution that can degrade the environment. This can lead to soil erosion, water pollution, and other forms of damage that can have severe consequences.

Deforestation

Overpopulation leads to an increased demand for housing, food, and resources, which can lead, among other things, to deforestation. We lose approximately 10 million hectares a year. This results in the loss of animal habitats and exacerbates climate change by reducing the amount of carbon dioxide that can be absorbed by plants.

Social Unrest

Overpopulation can lead to overcrowding, poverty, food insecurity, and other social issues. This can create tension between communities and countries as resources become increasingly scarce.

Loss of Biodiversity

In 2020, WWF reported that over the last 50 years, we have seen an average 68% decrease in the populations of mammals, birds, fish, reptiles, and amphibians. As habitats are destroyed to make way for human habitation, the diversity of wildlife decreases. This has a negative impact on the food chain and can threaten entire species with extinction.

Challenges Posed by Overpopulation on Sustainability

The challenges posed by overpopulation on sustainability are complex and require urgent attention. Here, we outline some of the most pressing issues.

Food Security

As the population continues to grow, there will be an increased demand for food. This can lead to shortages and higher prices in some countries, making it difficult for people to access nutritious meals.

Housing

Overpopulation can lead to overcrowding and a lack of resources, which makes it difficult for people to find adequate housing. This problem is particularly acute in developing countries where there is a lack of infrastructure and resources.

Education

Overpopulation can also create difficulties for students as there is limited access to schools and teachers. This hampers their ability to gain an education and limits their opportunities in the future.

Healthcare

According to World Bank and the World Health Organization (WHO), almost half of the world's population lacks access to essential care services. As more people require medical care, existing healthcare systems become overburdened and unable to provide adequate services. This can lead to a lack of access to essential medical care in some areas.

Pollution

With more people comes more waste and pollution, which can lead to water contamination, air pollution, and other environmental issues. This has a detrimental effect on the planet's ecosystems as well as human health. WHO estimates that pollution can be associated with 7 million premature deaths each year.

Solutions to Overpopulation and Sustainability Challenges

There are a number of solutions that can help to address the challenges posed by overpopulation on sustainability. These include:

Improved Education

Education is one of the most important tools for addressing overpopulation and its related challenges.

By educating people about family planning, contraception, population growth trends, and other relevant topics, we can empower individuals to make informed decisions about their reproductive health.

Moreover, education around sustainable development initiatives, such as conservation and renewable energy sources, can help create more environmentally conscious communities. This can lead to more efficient use of resources and less pollution.

Lastly, providing educational opportunities for disadvantaged people, such as those living in rural areas or refugee camps, can help to reduce poverty levels by creating job opportunities and improving access to healthcare.

Family Planning

Family planning is a critical tool for addressing overpopulation.

Through programmes promoting access to contraception, reproductive health education, gender equality and women's rights, we can empower individuals to make informed decisions about their lives and fertility.

As of 2023, the United Nations Population Fund reports that 257 million women are using ineffective or even potentially dangerous family planning methods, which impacts them, their families, and whole communities.

Family planning initiatives can lead to lower poverty levels as they help couples plan for the size of their families and ensure that resources are more evenly distributed among children. This can provide increased economic stability for entire communities.

Renewable Energy

A recent report by the International Energy Agency (IEA) suggests that the power sector is set for a "tipping point" on its carbon dioxide emissions in 2025, as renewables and other cleaner sources, including nuclear energy, are on track to cover most of the new global electricity demand.

That's great news, considered that renewable energy sources, such as solar, wind, and hydropower can help minimise our reliance on fossil fuels and create a more sustainable future. By investing in renewable energy initiatives, we can reduce our carbon footprint and protect the environment from further degradation. This way, the air quality and water supply can be improved, creating a healthier environment for everyone.

In addition, renewable energy can create job opportunities and improve access to electricity in some of the most remote areas in the world. This can have a positive effect on people's overall quality of life.

Sustainable Agriculture

Sustainable agriculture is a critical component of creating an environmentally conscious society.

By encouraging the use of organic farming practices and minimising chemical inputs, we can reduce soil erosion, water contamination, and other forms of environmental degradation. This will help to maintain the health of our ecosystems while also increasing crop yields in some areas.

Moreover, sustainable agriculture initiatives can create job opportunities for rural communities and provide access to nutritious food for everyone. This way, we can ensure that resources are shared more equitably among people around the world.

Conservation Efforts

Conservation efforts are essential for preserving the environment and protecting biodiversity.

Through initiatives such as creating protected areas, reforestation projects, and responsible hunting, we can create a safe space for wildlife to thrive while also reducing the pressure on ecosystems. This will help to maintain the balance of nature and ensure that there is enough food available for all species in an area.

In addition, conservation efforts can lead to increased tourism revenue which can be used to fund sustainable development initiatives in local communities.

Green Technology

Green technology is a key part of creating a more sustainable society. It refers to the use of renewable energy sources, efficient production processes, and other initiatives that reduce our reliance on natural resources.

By investing in green technology, we can create jobs while also reducing pollution levels. This will help to improve air quality and water supply while also providing economic stability for communities around the world.

In addition, green technology can lead to increased efficiency in manufacturing processes, which could result in reduced costs for consumers and lower prices for goods.

Awareness and Advocacy

Finally, it is crucial to raise awareness and advocate for solutions to the challenges posed by overpopulation on sustainability.

This can be achieved through campaigns aimed at educating people about the impacts of population growth, as well as lobbying governments and decision-makers to invest in sustainable initiatives. It is also important to maintain a dialogue with the public and engage them in conversations about how we can work together to create a better world.

By creating an informed and engaged citizenry, we can create solutions to overpopulation and its related challenges.

The challenges posed by overpopulation on sustainability are daunting, but they are not insurmountable. By taking the right steps, we can ensure that our planet remains a safe and healthy home for generations to come. This can help to make essential products more accessible for everyone.

Conclusion

The impact of overpopulation on sustainability is a critical issue that must be addressed. Unsustainable consumption and environmental degradation due to population growth can have disastrous consequences for the planet and all its inhabitants.

Fortunately, there are solutions that we can pursue to address these challenges, from improved education to sustainable agriculture practices.

With concerted effort, it is possible for us to create a more sustainable future – one in which our planet's resources are managed responsibly and used in ways that benefit everyone. As the world continues to grow more crowded, it is essential that we take decisive action now so that future generations will not suffer from the impacts of overpopulation on sustainability.

Overpopulation Is Not to Blame

Fixating on overpopulation places the blame for the climate emergency on the bodies of the most disadvantaged women in the global south, the very people who are most affected by its impact. It is overconsumption that is the issue – the wealthiest countries with the lowest levels of fertility produce the highest levels of the emissions that drive global heating.

As the UN Population Fund warns, a narrow focus on birth control risks reproductive injustice. A reproductive justice approach would ensure all women's sexual and reproductive rights are upheld while shifting the responsibility for addressing the emergency to those most responsible for it.

"Overconsumption, not overpopulation, is driving the climate crisis" by Naomi Delap, Guardian News & Media Limited, October 20, 2022.

Viewpoint 4

> *"Businesses create new jobs and produce wealth. But if they fail to act responsibly, they can also pose a threat to society and the environment."*

Corporations Push Overconsumption

Niloufar Fallah Shayan, Nasrin Mohabbati-Kalejahi, Sepideh Alavi, and Mohammad Ali Zahed

Corporations play a major role in the lives of everyday people. This includes influencing them to spend more money and buy more goods. In this viewpoint, researchers from Iran and the United States discuss the social responsibility that corporations have and the ways that acting in a responsible manner can lead to a more sustainable future for the planet and those who live on it.

As you read, consider the following questions:

1. Do you believe that corporations have certain social responsibilities?
2. What are some ways the COVID-19 pandemic affected global production and consumption?
3. How has the idea of Corporate Social Responsibility changed in response to other global events, such as major elections or natural disasters?

"Sustainable Development Goals (SDGs) as a Framework for Corporate Social Responsibility (CSR)" by Fallah Shayan N, Mohabbati-Kalejahi N, Alavi S and Zahed MA, MDPI, 21 January 2022.

Abstract

Corporate Social Responsibility (CSR) has been an articulated practice for over 7 decades. Still, most corporations lack an integrated framework to develop a strategic, balanced, and effective approach to achieving excellence in CSR. Considering the world's critical situation during the COVID-19 pandemic, such a framework is even more crucial now. We suggest subsuming CSR categories under Sustainable Development Goals (SDGs) be used and that they subsume CSR categories since SDGs are a comprehensive agenda designed for the whole planet. This study presents a new CSR drivers model and a novel comprehensive CSR model. Then, it highlights the advantages of integrating CSR and SDGs in a new framework. The proposed framework benefits from both CSR and SDGs, addresses current and future needs, and offers a better roadmap with more measurable outcomes.

Introduction

Businesses create new jobs and produce wealth. But if they fail to act responsibly, they can also pose a threat to society and the environment. Corporate Social Responsibility (CSR) can mitigate corporate damage by encouraging socially responsible, and environmentally-friendly, actions [1]. A CSR plan establishes a strategy to support socio-economic and environmental sustainability through management and stakeholder involvement [2]. An increasingly populated planet struggling with massive climate change problems provides evidence of why businesses should not engage in CSR from a solely local context since they exist within an interconnected world. Short-term corporate actions have irrefutable impacts on the environment, society, and economy which is why the long-term perspective of CSR is important for the health of the planet.

The current pandemic of COVID-19 has highlighted the significance of CSR. Humans are now more aware than ever of how connected everyone is around the globe, and how irresponsible action can wreak havoc for all. The Coronavirus began with just one person, spread through global travel and product transports, and in less than a year, it spread to nearly every country [3]. Social life has changed since the COVID-19 outbreak. The global stock market fluctuation, the quarantine measures, and social distancing were just some of the effects. Businesses are negatively impacted by the Corona Virus [4] such as temporary or permanent closures, layoffs [5], and cash flow constraints [6]. Such unexpected changes in the world highlight the importance of CSR. It could motivate companies to revise their approach to social responsibility, realizing that a simple mistake or irresponsible action would have a major impact worldwide. Meanwhile, corporations recognize the need to equip themselves with risk and emergency management tools for their own benefit as well as that of their society [7].

CSR played a huge role in the business world even before the start of the pandemic. Corporations have invested in socially responsible plans out of ethical and philanthropic purposes or financial ones for years. But not many of these plans were systematically designed. Each company scanned their society's issues and challenges, picked one or a few of the matters based on their own limited knowledge, and tried to make a small difference in a localized context. Most companies did not have the facilities to properly measure the final effects of their contributions. A well-designed framework, the most comprehensive one in the world, is proposed in this study to help companies structure their CSR plans. This framework is the SDGs mapped out by the United Nations (UN).

According to the United Nations [8], Sustainable Development is "the development which meets the needs of the present without compromising the ability of future generations to meet their own needs". SDGs consist of 17 goals, as illustrated in Tabe-2, over the period of 2015–2030. Individuals, communities, small businesses, and large corporations all benefit from the SDGs [9]. Global experts' knowledge and the opinions of governments, organizations, institutions, as well as the voices of millions of people were used to establish the SDGs. The 17 Sustainable Development goals are an ideal framework for CSR plans. In addition to addressing the same general purpose as CSR, which is the wellbeing of society, SDGs are based on the problems of the current and future world. The SDGs receive funding every year, and their impact has been substantial. The SDGs are already widely known and globally recognized, making this course of action an immediate opportunity. This study demonstrates how SDGs as a framework for CSR will benefit people, the planet, and corporations themselves. Additionally, the SDGs serve as a basis for the Global Reporting Initiative (GRI), the Community Development Program (CDP), the International Integrated Reporting Council (IIRC), and the Climate Disclosure Standards Board (CDSP). Corporations' contributions to the SDGs are disclosed by these institutions. Furthermore, these five standard-setting institutions have formally agreed to work together to develop a comprehensive report on corporate sustainability and corporate responsibility in September 2020 [10], that enhances CSR communication of firms if they are SDG-related.

This study offers a new perspective on CSR implementation: a perspective that results in worldwide and sustainable impacts. We first investigate CSR drivers in a way that no one has done before, and suggest CSR benefits for corporations on the basis of recent literature reviews then introduce a new model for CSR that integrates previous models and also adds new dimensions. Second, we introduce the SDGs and discuss their status and significant progress around the world based on the United Nations' annual reports. Finally, we discuss all 17 goals of the SDGs from the perspective of how they can benefit corporations, and propose our comprehensive framework for CSR implementation based on the SDGs.

Corporate Social Responsibility

Corporate Social Responsibility was formulated as a cohesive concept in the 1950s and expanded in the 1960s [11]. The debate was whether corporations should go beyond their own shareholders' value to support society's needs, or such effort was beyond corporations' responsibilities. To be effective, CSR must combine theory with practice. Fortunately, since the 1960s, both corporations and researchers have played a huge role in developing CSR [12].

CSR has a close relationship with a variety of terms and concepts that have evolved over time: Corporate sustainability [13], corporate citizenship [14], corporate responsibility [15], corporate social performance [16] corporate reputation [17,18], business ethics [19] and corporate philanthropy [20]. This article, however, will focus on the original concept.

Currently, the Coronavirus pandemic has highlighted the importance of businesses CSR strategies. In response to the crisis, some corporations remained loyal to their understanding of ethics, some "stepped up" and helped their society with all the means at their disposal, while some others took advantage of the situation and tried to gain short-term benefits [21]. The long-term consequences of such short-term profit-taking, however, can lead to reputation damage, or even worse, missing out on opportunities to improve their public image and credibility. Through the pandemic corporations have been forced to choose between helping society or focusing on their survival. Some companies have chosen to use SDGs as a guideline in order to create a balance between their own interests and society's wellbeing [22]. Some examples would be investments that generate stock returns [23,24] or investments in COVID-19 protection, prevention, treatment and rehabilitation [25] to offset the economic and health-related impacts of COVID.

With the global Coronavirus outbreak, the world has realized the importance of CSR more. As an example, in the case of many companies, supply chains are experiencing disruptions in supply, cancellation of orders, delayed payments, reductions in sales, and financial difficulties [26]. Under such circumstances, a portion of a corporation's CSR budget could be allocated to their supply chain partners in the form of loans or donations, which would be of great help until the crisis is over. In return, corporations keep their reliable suppliers and avoid transition costs and risks. Another example would be corporations that support their employees' health and financial status by preparing the infrastructure for them to work from home. As a result, employee satisfaction and trust increased, while the risk of employee loss was decreased. In this extraordinary period of time, companies are constantly reviewing their CSR strategies to determine what society expects from them [27].

We Can Change Our Habits without Changing the Planet's Population

Goal 12 [of the United Nations' Sustainable Development Goals] is about ensuring sustainable consumption and production patterns, which is key to sustain the livelihoods of current and future generations.

Our planet is running out of resources, but populations are continuing to grow. If the global population reaches 9.8 billion by 2050, the equivalent of almost three planets will be required to provide the natural resources needed to sustain current lifestyles.

We need to change our consumption habits, and shifting our energy supplies to more sustainable ones are one of the main changes we must make if we are going to reduce our consumption levels. However, global crises triggered a resurgence in fossil fuel subsidies, nearly doubling from 2020 to 2021.

We are seeing promising changes in industries, including the trend towards sustainability reporting being on the rise, almost tripling the amount of published sustainability over just a few years, showing increased levels of commitment and awareness that sustainability should be at the core of business practices.

Food waste is another sign of over consumption, and tackling food loss is urgent and requires dedicated policies, informed by data, as well as investments in technologies, infrastructure, education and monitoring. A staggering 931 million tons of food is wasted a year, despite a huge number of the global population going hungry.

Why do we need to change the way we consume?

Economic and social progress over the last century has been accompanied by environmental degradation that is endangering the very systems on which our future development and very survival depend.

A successful transition will mean improvements in resource efficiency, consideration of the entire life cycle of economic activities, and active engagement in multilateral environmental agreements

What needs to change?

There are many aspects of consumption that with simple changes can have a big impact on society as a whole.

Governments need to implement and enforce policies and regulations that include measures such as setting targets for reducing waste generation, promoting circular economy practices, and supporting sustainable procurement policies

Transitioning to a circular economy involves designing products for longevity, repairability, and recyclability. It also involves promoting practices such as reusing, refurbishing, and recycling products to minimize waste and resource depletion.

Individuals can also adopt more sustainable lifestyles – this can involve consuming less, choosing products with lower environmental impacts, and reducing the carbon footprint of day-to-day activities

How can I help as a business?

It's in businesses' interest to find new solutions that enable sustainable consumption and production patterns. A better understanding of environmental and social impacts of products and services is needed, both of product life cycles and how these are affected by use within lifestyles.

Innovation and design solutions can both enable and inspire individuals to lead more sustainable lifestyles, reducing impacts and improving well-being.

How can I help as a consumer?

There are two main ways to help:

Reducing your waste and

Being thoughtful about what you buy and choosing a sustainable option whenever possible.

Ensure you don't throw away food, and reduce your consumption of plastic—one of the main pollutants of the ocean. Carrying a reusable bag, refusing to use plastic straws, and recycling plastic bottles are good ways to do your part every day.

Making informed purchases also helps. By buying from sustainable and local sources you can make a difference as well as exercising pressure on businesses to adopt sustainable practices.

"Goal 12: Ensure sustainable consumption and production patterns" by United Nations

Periodical and Internet Sources Bibliography

The following articles have been selected to supplement the diverse views presented in this chapter.

Ali Borji, "The Overconsumption Crisis: Causes, Consequences, and Solutions," Medium, December 5, 2024. medium.com/@aliborji/the-overconsumption-crisis-causes-consequences-and-solutions-55766c0eb0ac.

Chip Colwell, "Too Much Stuff: Can We Solve Our Addiction to Consumerism?," The Guardian, November 28, 2023. www.theguardian.com/environment/2023/nov/28/too-much-stuff-can-we-solve-our-addiction-to-consumerism.

Elena Dawkins, Karin André, Katarina Axelsson, Lise Benoist, Åsa Gerger Swartling, and Åsa Persson, "Advancing sustainable consumption at the local government level: A literature review," ScienceDirect, September 10, 2019. www.sciencedirect.com/science/article/pii/S0959652619317044.

Ramon Duran and Brian Green, "ESG and Corporations that Promote Overconsumption of Resources," Santa Clara Markkula Center for Applied Ethics, October 20, 2022. www.scu.edu/environmental-ethics/resources/esg-and-corporations-that-promote-overconsumption-of-resources/?.

Elizabeth Oldfield, "Corporations vs. Consumers: Who Is Really to Blame for Climate Change?," University of Manchester, July 7, 2022. sites.manchester.ac.uk/global-social-challenges/2022/07/07/corporations-vs-consumers-who-is-really-to-blame-for-climate-change/.

"Over-Consumption in the World's Richest Countries Is Destroying Children's Environments Globally, New Report Says," UNICEF, May 23, 2022. www.unicef.org/press-releases/over-consumption-worlds-richest-countries-destroying-childrens-environments-globally.

Cody Peluso, "What Causes Overconsumption and Overshoot?," Population Media Center, January 18, 2024. www.populationmedia.org/the-latest/why-does-the-earth-overshoot.

Emily Shu, "No, Corporations Aren't the Only Ones Responsible for Your Overconsumption," *The Voice,* April 30, 2024. ihsvoice.com/2024/04/30/no-corporations-arent-the-only-ones-responsible-for-your-overconsumption/.

Chapter 3

Can We Solve the Problem of Overconsumption?

Chapter Preface

Overconsumption affects the environment, the economy, and the well-being of people around the world. It is a pressing problem. What, if anything, can we do about it?

Some people believe that with the right mix of innovation, education, and policy, overconsumption can be reduced or even reversed. They point to growing interest in sustainability, the rise of the circular economy, and lifestyle movements like minimalism and zero-waste living. Others argue that real change is unlikely without a complete shift in cultural values and global economic priorities—something much harder to achieve.

This chapter explores a range of proposed solutions, from individual behavior changes to large-scale economic reforms. It also raises tough questions: Will corporations act responsibly without being forced to? Are people willing to give up convenience and comfort for the sake of long-term sustainability? Which proposed solutions are viable, and which are simply putting a band-aid on a bullet wound?

By presenting differing viewpoints, this chapter encourages readers to consider what solutions are realistic, what sacrifices may be required, and whether solving overconsumption is a matter of personal choice, collective responsibility, or both.

Viewpoint 1

> *"By misleading the public to believe that a company or other entity is doing more to protect the environment than it is, greenwashing promotes false solutions to the climate crisis that distract from and delay concrete and credible action."*

Greenwashing Is Part of the Problem

United Nations

As support for sustainability grows, many companies have realized that being environmentally friendly will help them attract customers. The problem is that many companies are not willing to make the changes that would make their products truly sustainable. In this viewpoint, the United Nations explains what greenwashing is and why it is problematic.

As you read, consider the following questions:

1. What are some examples of greenwashing you've encountered in your own life?
2. Why is greenwashing not just unhelpful but actively harmful?
3. What are some ways you can spot and avoid greenwashing?

Greenwashing presents a significant obstacle to tackling climate change. By misleading the public to believe that a company or other entity is doing more to protect the environment than it is, greenwashing promotes false solutions to the climate crisis that distract from and delay concrete and credible action.

Greenwashing manifests itself in several ways – some more obvious than others. Tactics include:

- Claiming to be on track to reduce a company's polluting emissions to net zero when no credible plan is actually in place.
- Being purposely vague or non-specific about a company's operations or materials used.
- Applying intentionally misleading labels such as "green" or "eco-friendly," which do not have standard definitions and can be easily misinterpreted.
- Implying that a minor improvement has a major impact or promoting a product that meets the minimum regulatory requirements as if it is significantly better than the standard.
- Emphasizing a single environmental attribute while ignoring other impacts.
- Claiming to avoid illegal or non-standard practices that are irrelevant to a product.
- Communicating the sustainability attributes of a product in isolation of brand activities (and vice versa) – e.g. a garment made from recycled materials that is produced in a high-emitting factory that pollutes the air and nearby waterways.

Why care about greenwashing, and how does it relate to climate change?

The science is clear: greenhouse gas emissions, such as carbon and methane, from human activities are wrapping the Earth in a blanket of pollution that has warmed the planet and led to severe impacts such as more intense storms, droughts, floods and wildfires.

To limit climate change and preserve a livable planet, emissions need to be cut nearly in half by 2030 and reduced to net zero by

2050. Every fraction of a degree of warming matters and, as put by the former chair of the High-Level Expert Group on the Net-Zero Emissions Commitments of Non-State Entities, "the planet cannot afford delays, excuses, or more greenwashing".

Greenwashing undermines credible efforts to reduce emissions and address the climate crisis. Through deceptive marketing and false claims of sustainability, greenwashing misleads consumers, investors, and the public, hampering the trust, ambition, and action needed to bring about global change and secure a sustainable planet.

How is the UN tackling greenwashing?

Since the adoption of the Paris Agreement in 2015, an increasing number of companies have pledged to reduce their greenhouse gas emissions to net zero - a level where any remaining emissions would be absorbed by forests, the ocean or other "carbon sinks." However, those claims are often based on questionable plans, including emissions offsetting and "insetting" – rather than actual emission cuts. As such, the transparency and integrity of such claims remain critically low and risk creating a failure to deliver urgent climate action.

In response to the rise in greenwashing in net-zero pledges, the Secretary-General established a High-Level Expert Group tasked with developing stronger and clearer standards for net-zero emissions pledges by companies, financial institutions, cities and regions, and speed up their implementation. In its report "Integrity Matters," the Expert Group outlined ten recommendations for credible, accountable net-zero pledges and detailed the necessary considerations for each stage towards achieving net zero and addressing the climate crisis.

Following the report, UN Climate Change published a Recognition and Accountability Framework and Draft Implementation Plan to begin operationalizing the expert group's recommendations, improve transparency and maximize the credibility of climate action pledges, plans and transition progress.

To further accelerate action and hear from "first movers and doers," the UN Secretary-General convened a Climate Ambition Summit at the UN Headquarters in New York on 20 September 2023, designed along three tracks: ambition, credibility, and implementation - leaving "no room for back-sliders, greenwashers, blame-shifters or repackaging of announcements of previous years".

In his pivotal speech on World Environment Day 2024, the Secretary-General called for a global ban on fossil fuel advertising and urged creative agencies to stop helping fossil fuel companies in greenwashing.

What can you do?

Learn more: as a consumer, understanding the common greenwashing tactics and what constitutes sustainable practices and products is crucial to recognizing and avoiding greenwashing.

Spend wisely: when possible, take time to research and choose products from companies who use resources responsibly and are committed to cutting their emissions and waste. A great place to start your research is to check if the company is aligned with any of the UN's climate and sustainability initiatives, such as the UNFCCC's Race to Zero or Fashion Industry Charter for Climate Action, and the UN Alliance for Sustainable Fashion, among others.

Consider a product's lifecycle: when evaluating a product, it is crucial to consider its entire life cycle, starting from the extraction of raw materials to its eventual disposal, while also taking into account the environmental consequences associated with its materials and packaging.

Look for transparency and accountability: it is often hard to know if companies are on track to meet their net zero commitments, and the absence of standardized and comparable data makes it hard to assess progress. The UN-backed credibility standards and criteria make it possible to reward leading entities taking bold, credible steps.

Consumers Have Choices

Consumer choice can drive positive change in industries by demanding social responsibility from their producers. Conscious consumerism can invoke practices like ethical sourcing and sustainable design.

According to a 2022 study, 66% of global consumers rank sustainability in their top five considerations when making a purchase decision. There is plenty of data making it clear that consumers are increasingly favouring sustainable goods. This has driven some companies to be more conscious of their environmental footprint and work on sustainable approaches in response to consumer demand.

It is a clear show of the power of consumer choice. But is that enough to push companies to drastically lower their polluting emissions and produce less e-waste?

Bottlenecks to making a sustainable choice

Consumer demand can influence market trends only to a certain extent. There are several larger issues ranging from the need for government incentives and regulations to international cooperation in policy making. The high price of some sustainable goods might be a factor impacting their choice or the lack of availability of sustainable goods might be another.

Yet another factor is the deleterious effect of exaggerated environmental claims or greenwashing. If the green claims of a brand seem insincere, it is easy for the consumer to lose trust in its products. Consequently, there is a need for more information and clarity on the sustainable practices of a product or a company advertising them.

Influence via digital media

There are other ways to foster sustainability in the market. When it comes to creating access and awareness, digital technology can be a huge driver.

In today's information driven, socially connected world, another key factor is digital influence. Advertising via social media platforms or gaining an edge on recommendations via apps and websites are effective ways of gaining customers. An ethically responsible application could provide environmentally conscious recommendations.

Some online shopping websites have started suggesting second-hand alternatives for the products the customer is searching for. Some rate the products on their platform by their degree of sustainability; others rely on verified customer reviews in highlighting different social or environmental impacts of the products.

But having access to information isn't enough, it needs to be trustable. While individual customer reviews can be illuminating, they still are not always a reliable assessment of a product's quality or other aspects such as sustainable design. How can a market achieve that?

Building trust

Once it's established that a sizeable segment of the market demands sustainable products, often producers compete for attention by highlighting their sustainable practices. However sometimes advertising wars can give way to exaggerated claims. To dispel doubts about sustainability claims from a manufacturer, obtaining certifications from a reliable, independent body proves to be an effective solution. IECQ, the IEC Quality Assessment System, offers ecodesign certification for products.

Companies can use this certification as proof of the veracity of their environmental claims, thus building credibility with customers. Ecodesign focuses on the environmental impacts of a product over its entire life cycle. Introducing environmental considerations into the scope of the design and development process of that product aims to reduce environmental impacts and supports a circular economy.

Getting this certification enables not only manufacturers, but also consumers, to make a well-informed choice. Simultaneously, they foster competition reliant on best practices for eco-friendly approaches, encouraging other companies to follow suit.

Need for more regulations

Providing verifiable information to help make better choices is not just ethically responsible, it also provides a competitive edge to companies in a market where people prioritize sustainability.

To truly facilitate the shift to a global circular economy, there is a need for international cooperation. More should be done in regulations to incentivize manufacturers to embrace sustainable practices and to make more sustainable choices accessible. Such regulations, coupled with consumers choosing sustainable options, can be formidable drivers for a more environmentally conscious market.

"The rise of conscious consumerism" by IEC Editorial Team, March 22, 2024.

Viewpoint 2

> *"Economic growth may be a fairytale to some, but to the over 700 million people worldwide living in conditions of extreme poverty, it is not a fairytale but a necessity."*

Economic Growth Is as Important as Environmentalism

Steven Cohen

Many solutions to overconsumption and the climate crisis focus on urging people to buy less. However, in this viewpoint, Dr. Steven Cohen argues that this would cause an economic crisis that would, like the climate crisis, disproportionately affect the poorest and most vulnerable people in society. Instead, Cohen believes we need to find solutions that prioritize economic growth in ways that do not harm the planet. Dr. Steven Cohen is the senior vice dean of Columbia University's School of Professional Studies.

As you read, consider the following questions:

1. According to the viewpoint, how can economic growth happen without environmental damage?
2. What kind of technology can help reduce overconsumption?
3. How are young people leading the movement to decrease overconsumption and pollution?

"Climate Change and Economic Consumption" by Steven Cohen, Columbia University, September 30, 2019. Reprinted by permission.

Like many environmentalists, I am impressed and inspired by Greta Thunberg. Her direct and clear message on the need to respond to climate change is a lesson to all of us. While I agree with most of her message, I take issue with some of it. Let's consider a portion of her recent talk at the U.N. whose message went viral:

> "You have stolen my dreams and my childhood with your empty words. And yet I'm one of the lucky ones. People are suffering. People are dying. Entire ecosystems are collapsing. We are in the beginning of a mass extinction, and all you can talk about is money and fairy tales of eternal economic growth. How dare you!"

Economic growth may be a fairytale to some, but to the over 700 million people worldwide living in conditions of extreme poverty, it is not a fairytale but a necessity. And for the long-term political stability of the world, the elimination of all poverty and reduced income inequality will likely depend on both increased taxation of wealth along with economic growth. But what can and must change is the nature of that economic activity and its impact on the planet.

Put simply, eating a meal at a restaurant is an economic activity, but the environmental impact of a salad is likely to be less than of a steak. A ride on the subway has a lower carbon footprint than a trip to the same destination in an SUV unless the SUV is electric and shared with six other passengers. We can swim in the ocean and sit on a beach or ride a jet-ski and return to the cabin cruiser. The first activity is environmentally benign, the second much less so. It's all consumption and any lifestyle of activity, excitement and learning requires resources. But even though all consumption and production can be measured in dollars, each dollar's impact on the environment is not equal.

One of my long-term concerns about environmental politics has always been the tendency of some environmentalists to focus on the negative and what must be sacrificed to save the planet. I prefer to focus on the positive and the advantages of a sustainable lifestyle. Politically, telling people what they can't have is a losing strategy. Rather than making people feel guilty if they like to eat meat, I think it's much more useful to demonstrate how delicious the alternatives can be.

There are many varieties of consumption and production and economic growth does not automatically translate into additional pollutant load on the planet. In the United States and other developed nations, we have decoupled the growth of the GDP from the growth of pollution. We do it by applying technology to control the negative impacts of other technologies. We also do it by creating technologies that perform similar functions with less environmental impact—for example, the technology of streaming movies compared to delivering the same product with video cassettes. The pollution control business, renewable energy business and energy efficiency business are real profit-making businesses. They create a product that we all need: cleaner air, water and land.

We need more of these businesses, not fewer of them and their existence is very real and no fantasy.

As we get more technically and managerially proficient, we will develop a growing capacity to close the loop on material production from start to finish. More and more new goods will be made of recycled rather than newly mined or manufactured materials. As our economy decarbonizes these energy-intensive recycling processes will have a lower and lower impact on greenhouse gas emissions. We need technology, organizational capacity, human ingenuity and political will to make this happen. To move a massive economy away from practices that harm environmental quality we need additional federal regulation and both financial incentives and disincentives to hardwire sustainability management into organizational life. The ideological intensity and institutional dysfunction in the United States national government is hindering this effort, but fortunately, there are governments in other parts of the world and in America outside our capital that understand the crisis of global sustainability. In America, our local governments must deliver real daily services and have managed to maintain that streak of pragmatism that still seems to dominate the culture of our way of life. Adapting to climate change may be called flood control in some places, but the result is the same.

More important than what's going on in government, there is evidence that we are in a massive cultural shift as young people entering organizational life and the world of work are demanding that organizations pay attention to their environmental impact. In our brain-based economy, the most talented young people have the leverage to make demands of their elders and they are doing just that. Fortunately, it's not culture alone that's changing but the cost structure of reducing environmental impact. As Chris Martin and Millicent Dent recently observed in *Bloomberg*:

> "It's time to stop crediting corporate sustainability efforts as acts of altruism. For big business, protecting the environment often means padding the bottom line. Nike Inc. has come up with a way to weave more efficiently, reducing the raw material and labor time needed to make each shoe. That has kept more than 3.5 million pounds of waste from reaching landfills since 2012. But the good news doesn't stop with the environmental impact. The company is spending less on transportation, materials and waste disposal.... Tech giants have spent billions of dollars on solar and wind power, cutting greenhouse-gas emissions and energy expenditures at the same time. Alphabet Inc.'s Google, Amazon and Facebook Inc. are now some of the largest buyers of green power in America. Turns out it's not just easy being green—it's also profitable."

The idea that we can grow our economy without harming the environment is not accepted by everyone, but more people are beginning to understand the concept. The importance of this growth is underscored by its political necessity. Poverty and its accompanying hopelessness are the breeding grounds for political extremism, political violence and terrorism. People with an ownership stake in society don't tend to want to blow it up. Those who perceive they have little to lose and maintain a deep sense of grievance are one source of political violence. Another source are power-mad rulers who attack their own people to preserve their authority. I make both of these points to indicate that climate change is far from the only problem that humanity faces. The pain and suffering of warfare is also a real and present danger. Political stability in the modern global economy is enhanced by economic growth. Political instability is often the result of the absence of that growth.

We need to address climate change with care and precision to ensure that the steps we take to decarbonize our economy promote growth and do not prevent it. As the technology of renewable energy, energy efficiency and energy storage has advanced it has lowered its price and become cost competitive with fossil fuels. We can anticipate that these advances will continue and that the best managed organizations will gravitate toward these energy sources for their economic as well as their environmental benefits. These benefits are not a fantasy.

What I wish was a fantasy was the slow-moving national governments that Greta Thunberg addressed at the United Nations. Their temporizing, insincere platitudes fool no one. It would be far better if they explained the real trade-offs they face. Here in New York City, the resources we would use to decarbonize or adapt to climate change must be traded off against resources that are also needed for homeless children, education, health care, senior services and mass transit. We can and must do more to move up the pace of decarbonization, but we will only achieve that goal by cutting out the symbolic rhetoric and getting down to the hard, daily work of changing the way we operate our homes, neighborhoods and organizations. Climate change requires nothing less than transforming the nature of economic production and consumption: Not to consume less, but to consume without destroying the planet that sustains us.and demand gap is to improve the forecasting of what consumers will or won't buy.

Fast Fashion Is a Serious Problem

The pursuit of "material wealth" has a complex relationship with overconsumption, especially clothing. And we live in a society where consumers are highly influenced by societal pressure and advertising; where the idea of having everything irrespective of need has led to a wasteful consumption culture.

I understand overconsumption through the vicious loop set up by the fast fashion industry. The rapid production of cheap clothing that is advertised as seasonal ranges and must-haves by brands encourages people to get their hands on everything. This idea of staying "in-trend" leads to mindless consumption of clothing.

But consumers can't be blamed alone since overproduction is as much a part of the problem.

It doesn't come as a surprise that the fashion industry is one of the most polluting, with over 100 billion garments produced each year and 92 million tonnes ending up in landfills based on the data shared by earth.org.

The Fashion Transparency Index 2023 explains that mitigating fashion waste remains the elephant in the room with a 3% increase in fashion brands not disclosing their annual production volumes (88% in 2023 compared to 85% in 2022).

The crux, though, is that both overproduction and overconsumption lead to heaps of waste being generated. The excess inventory often finds its way to landfills, is incinerated or finds its way to countries like Uganda which serves as a second-hand clothing market.

Recently, there have been discussions about the ban on importing second-hand clothing into Uganda in an effort to stimulate the country's own textiles industry.

At the other end of the spectrum, some retailers and companies are putting in efforts to curb this wasteful production. For instance, wood-based speciality fibre company Lenzing Group adds up to 20% recycled raw material content from post-consumer textile waste to its Ecovera branded viscose fibres.

Industry veterans are also debating whether artificial intelligence (AI) can solve fashion's overproduction problem and be a key money-making opportunity for both fashion brands and manufacturers.

Ganesh Subramanian, CEO of fashion software company Stylumia suggests a radical solution to overconsumption. Subramanian argues that in the world as we know it today, the only way to solve the supply and demand gap is to improve the forecasting of what consumers will or won't buy.

But the question is, can technology really end the wasteful culture that we "humans" have either unknowingly or knowingly accepted and continue to market?

"Week in review: Clothing overproduction, overconsumption and can tech fix it?" by Shemona Safaya, Verdict Media, September 4, 2023.

Viewpoint 3

"People are becoming increasingly aware of our planet's finite resources and the consequences of overconsumption. As a result, they seek products and services that align with their values and positively impact the world."

We All Need to Be Conscious Consumers

Olwen van Dijk-Hildebrand

Although advertisers tend to push the idea that their products are necessary – for life, for happiness, for social status, or to fill some other niche in a person's life – more and more people are starting to question the choices they make when shopping. The term "conscious consumerism" describes a movement toward assessing whether a business or product aligns with a person's values before spending money on it. In this viewpoint, Olwen van Dijk-Hildebrand explains how this movement is changing the way people shop. Van Dijk-Hildebrand is the head of operations at 2Stallions, a digital marketing agency.

As you read, consider the following questions:

1. Why is a circular economy so important?
2. How can we overcome some of the barriers to implementing this type of economy?
3. What are some examples of the three pillars of a circular economy that you can implement in your own life?

In recent years, a powerful force has emerged in the world of business: the conscious consumer. These individuals desire products and services that meet their needs and are deeply committed to sustainability and ethical practices. Their purchasing decisions are no longer solely based on price and convenience but also on businesses' impact on the environment, society, and future generations.

Understanding the Conscious Consumer

As sustainability has become a global issue, consumer attitudes and behaviours have evolved in response. What was once a niche movement has now become mainstream, with more and more individuals prioritising sustainability in their purchasing decisions.

One of the key drivers behind this shift is a growing understanding of consumption's environmental and social impact. People are becoming increasingly aware of our planet's finite resources and the consequences of overconsumption. As a result, they seek products and services that align with their values and positively impact the world.

Sustainability now influences every stage of the consumer journey, from product research and comparison to purchasing. Consumers seek information about a company's environmental policies, supply chain practices, and overall commitment to sustainability. They want to support businesses that align with their values and positively impact society.

When it comes to product research, consumers are no longer solely focused on price and quality. They also consider the environmental and social implications of their choices.

For example, when looking for a new smartphone, consumers may research the manufacturing process to ensure it is environmentally friendly and that workers are treated fairly. This shift in consumer behaviour has led to an increase in demand for sustainable and ethically produced products.

Furthermore, consumers are now more conscious of a product's entire lifecycle. They want to know if a product is recyclable or will end up in a landfill after use. This awareness has led to increased popularity of products designed with circularity in mind, meaning they can be easily recycled or repurposed at the end of their life.

Another aspect of consumer behaviour influenced by sustainability is the rise of the sharing economy. Instead of owning and consuming products individually, consumers now embrace sharing resources. This can be seen in the popularity of ride-sharing services like Uber and accommodation-sharing platforms like Airbnb. By sharing resources, consumers can reduce waste and minimise their environmental impact.

Moreover, sustainability has also impacted how consumers perceive and interact with brands. Companies that prioritise sustainability and demonstrate a genuine commitment to environmental and social responsibility are more likely to gain the trust and loyalty of consumers. In contrast, businesses seen as environmentally irresponsible or engaged in unethical practices may face backlash and declining consumer support.

Overall, the intersection of sustainability and consumer behaviour is a complex and multifaceted phenomenon. Consumers are increasingly aware of the environmental and social impact of their choices and are actively seeking sustainable alternatives. This shift in consumer behaviour has the potential to drive positive change and encourage businesses to adopt more sustainable practices. As sustainability continues to gain prominence, consumer attitudes and behaviours will likely continue to evolve, shaping the future of the marketplace.

The Impact of Conscious Consumerism on Businesses

The rise of conscious consumerism has forced businesses to adapt and rethink their strategies. It is no longer enough to simply provide a quality product or service. Companies must demonstrate their commitment to sustainability and ensure transparency in their practices.

Adapting business strategies for the conscious consumer requires a holistic approach. This includes incorporating sustainable practices into all operations, from sourcing raw materials to manufacturing processes. It also involves communicating these efforts to consumers clearly and transparently, building trust and loyalty.

Transparency has emerged as a key element of sustainable business practices. Conscious consumers want to know where their products are coming from, how they are made, and their impact on the world. By providing this information upfront, businesses can build customer trust and differentiate themselves in the market.

The Future of Sustainability as a Market Force

As conscious consumerism continues to gain momentum, its impact on the market is projected to grow. It is no longer a passing trend but a permanent shift in consumer attitudes and behaviour. Businesses that fail to recognise and adapt to this shift risk being left behind.

Looking ahead, several predicted trends in conscious consumerism exist. As consumers become more informed and demanding, the demand for sustainable products and services is expected to increase. As a result, businesses will need to invest in innovation and develop sustainable alternatives that meet consumer needs without compromising on quality or functionality.

Furthermore, the long-term effects of sustainability on the market are likely to be significant. As businesses shift towards sustainable practices, industries will be pressured to become more environmentally and socially responsible. This will require collaboration and innovation on a global scale as businesses work together to find solutions to complex challenges.

In Conclusion

The conscious consumer's rise and commitment to sustainability has transformed the business landscape. Businesses can no longer ignore their impact on the world. To succeed in this new era, companies must understand and embrace the values of the conscious consumer, adapting their strategies and practices accordingly. By prioritising transparency, sustainability, and ethical practices, businesses can align with the values of conscious consumers and contribute to a more sustainable future.

Periodical and Internet Sources Bibliography

The following articles have been selected to supplement the diverse views presented in this chapter.

Shannon Cook, "How Can Sustainable Marketing Help Fight Overconsumption?," BusinessBecause, July 30, 2021. www.businessbecause.com/news/insights/7758/sustainable-marketing-overconsumption.

Quantanite Marketing, "The Power of Conscious Consumerism: Making Informed Choices for a Better Future," Quantanite, June 19, 2023. www.quantanite.com/blog/the-power-of-conscious-consumerism-making-informed-choices-for-a-better-future/.

Stephanie Ng, "Easy Ways Individuals Can Reduce Consumption," Resonance, April 8, 2024. www.resonanceglobal.com/blog/easy-ways-individuals-can-reduce-consumption.

"The 'De-Influencing' Trend Tackles Overconsumption and Its Harm On the Environment," NPR, February 25, 2024. www.npr.org/2024/02/25/1233819687/the-de-influencing-trend-tackles-overconsumption-and-its-harm-on-the-environment.

Noah Smith, "People Are Realizing That Degrowth Is Bad," Noahpinion, September 6, 2021. www.noahpinion.blog/p/people-are-realizing-that-degrowth.

Ksenija Stokuca, "A False Necessity: The Truth Behind Conscious Consumerism," Medium, October 11, 2021. medium.com/writ-150-at-usc-fall-2020/a-false-necessity-the-truth-behind-conscious-consumerism-42e5eda16c81.

Ana Birliga Sutherland, "Less Is More? Degrowth, Green Growth and the Future of Our Economy," Circle Economy, March 27, 2024. www.circle-economy.com/blog/less-is-more-degrowth-green-growth-and-the-future-of-our-economy.

Dani Rae Wascher, "Sustainable Solutions to Overconsumption Challenges in Modern Marketing," February 27, 2024. phys.org/news/2024-02-sustainable-solutions-overconsumption-modern.html.

Chapter 4

Is Consumerism without Overconsumption Possible?

Chapter Preface

Overconsumption is often treated as the natural consequence of consumerism, but how accurate is this view? Is it possible to enjoy the benefits of a consumer-driven economy without contributing to the waste, pollution, and social costs that come with excessive consumption?

This chapter explores whether a balance can be struck between buying and responsibility. Supporters of ethical consumerism argue that we can shop in ways that align with our values—by choosing sustainable products, supporting local businesses, and avoiding companies with harmful practices. They believe consumer culture doesn't have to be destructive if people are informed, intentional, and mindful of their impact.

Others are more skeptical. They argue that the system itself depends on overconsumption to survive. Even "green" or "ethical" products, they say, are often part of a marketing strategy that still encourages people to buy more. From this perspective, the problem isn't just *what* we consume, but the idea that constant consumption is necessary for happiness or progress.

This chapter invites readers to examine whether consumerism can be reimagined—or if true sustainability requires stepping outside the consumer mindset altogether.

Viewpoint 1

"On the hypothetical day the world stops shopping, carbon emissions plummet; the skies turn a deeper blue; and with no ads polluting smartphone screens our minds become as clear as the bottle-free oceans in which whales swim merrily."

To Stop Overconsuming, We Must Stop Shopping

Jamie Waters

Some people say that the problem of overconsumption is so serious that it requires an equally serious solution: stop shopping as much as possible. In this viewpoint, Jamie Waters talks to JB MacKinnon, the author of The Day the World Stops Shopping, *and discusses his ideas about how people can stop overconsuming. Waters is a freelance writer.*

As you read, consider the following questions:

1. How would the world be different if we decentered consumerism?
2. Is it possible for everyone to implement MacKinnon's ideas?

"Overconsumption and the environment: should we all stop shopping?" by Jamie Waters, Guardian News & Media, May 30, 2021. Reprinted by permission.

3. In what ways is MacKinnon's opinion more complex and nuanced than "just stop shopping"?

I fear I'm in JB MacKinnon's bad books. Halfway through our Zoom interview, I tilt my camera to adjust to the setting sun—but from this new angle, an e-commerce box can be spotted over my shoulder. Its barcode glows in the fading light, a totem of 21st-century materialism presiding over our call.

MacKinnon is too polite to say anything, but he can't be thrilled by my cardboard companion. After all, the Canadian bestselling author and journalist is on a mission to get us to buy a lot less stuff. *The Day the World Stops Shopping*, his new book, explores what might happen if the world transformed into a society that does not revolve around purchasing, one in which our primary role is not as consumers and our credit cards are not our most commonly deployed tools.

His "thought experiment" plays out like a Ridley Scott sci-fi epic—or perhaps a scene from the pandemic. On the hypothetical day the world stops shopping, carbon emissions plummet; the skies turn a deeper blue; and with no ads polluting smartphone screens our minds become as clear as the bottle-free oceans in which whales swim merrily. There's also chaos. Shops shut, production lines grind to a halt and millions of factory workers lose their jobs. The global economy nosedives so severely it makes the 2008 recession seem like a blip. "It would be a shock so great that it would seem to bend time itself," MacKinnon writes.

The only thing fantastical about his vision is the timeframe: rather than ceasing all shopping overnight he thinks we should, in reality, restructure society over several years to support a sustained reduction in the amount we consume.

He sees this as an obvious, if difficult, fix to a big problem. Consumption—of fast fashion, flights, Black Friday-discounted gadgets—has become the primary driver of ecological crisis. We are devouring the planet's resources at a rate 1.7 times faster than it can regenerate. The US population is 60% larger than it was in 1970, but consumer spending is up 400% (adjusted for inflation)—and other rich nations, including the UK, aren't much better. "Many people would like to see the world consume fewer resources, yet we constantly avoid the most obvious means of achieving that," says MacKinnon. "When people buy less stuff, you get immediate drops in emissions, resource consumption and pollution, unlike anything we've achieved with green technology." That's not to mention the impact materialism has on our mental health, inducing feelings of inadequacy and envy, and encouraging a culture of overworking.

His is an impassioned call to arms, for the sake of our planet and our wellbeing. But how feasible is it for all the world's citizens to swap Amazon baskets for a simple agrarian life? More pointedly, do we want to? Does MacKinnon's vision represent an enlightened Shangri-La—or a primitive dystopia?

"This is the best opportunity in the past 30 years to bring consumption back to the centre of the political discourse," says MacKinnon, speaking from his home in Vancouver. He's pensive, with piercing blue eyes. Indeed, the pandemic has given people pause to think about "how they consume, what their relationship with stuff should look like and what is deeply valuable in their lives," he says. "I don't think anybody is going to say that having a bunch of home-workout gear was as satisfying as being able to have contact with friends, family and neighbours."

Many of us still shopped—Amazon enjoyed record-breaking global revenues of $386bn in 2020—but, stripped of opportunities for parading possessions in front of others, there was a widespread rethink in why we buy and wear things. "For women, particularly, the idea that they don't constantly have to be messaging and positioning through their dress was interesting," he says. "Women saying they're never going to wear jeans or bras again—these are interesting individual reckonings."

Nonetheless, as much of the world begins to reopen, there are rallying cries to boost the economy by opening our wallets.

Shopping has been cast as a positive act, retail therapy a civic duty. "All the narratives are building around a new Roaring 20s, a hedonistic binge, taking revenge on the virus with our consumption," says MacKinnon. "But I think a lot of us are going to feel uncomfortable and disquieted, to the point of despair, as we remember what the fully revved-up consumer culture looks like."

He wants us to act on that discomfort. But he's not suggesting we live entirely off the land. In his hypothetical model he applies a 25% reduction in consumption—a figure "modest enough to be possible, dramatic enough to be earth-shattering"—and while he won't specify a figure when discussing what our real-world efforts should be in the coming years, something in this ballpark might well be the goal.

That doesn't just mean fewer physical things; it's also less electricity, travel and eating out. "Basically $1 spent is a consumption dollar; I'm not fussed whether it's spent on a canoe or a powerboat," he says. "If you want a rule of thumb for how much impact you're having as a consumer, the best one is: how much money are you spending? If it's increasing, you're probably increasing your impact; if it's lowering, you're probably lowering your impact."

How might a lower-consuming society look? Everything is reoriented because people, brands and governments are no longer striving for economic growth. Individuals are more self-sufficient, growing food, mending things and embracing wabi-sabi, the Japanese concept of imperfect aesthetics (think patched-up pockets or chipped ceramics). Brands produce fewer but better-quality goods, while governments ban planned obsolescence (the practice of producing items to only function for a set period of time), stick "durability" labels on items so shoppers can be assured of longevity, and introduce tax subsidies so it's cheaper to repair something than to bin it and buy a new version.

Why has such an approach never before been attempted on a broad, society-wide scale? MacKinnon rejects my suggestion that perhaps consumerism is hard-wired into human nature, but says it is "deeply ingrained" in society and it's "much easier for us to think, 'Let's make all these cars run on solar power instead of gas,' rather than, 'How do we end up with fewer cars?'" Plus, he says, "to some extent there was a point where we gave in to the idea that lowering consumption could not be a solution, because it inevitably results in economic collapse."

Well, doesn't it? Were we all to stop shopping overnight it would be disastrous, he admits, but if we built a new system, it could support a surprisingly robust economy. "If you're producing durable goods, you still need considerable labour. Then there's the secondhand market, the repair of products, taking items back in and recomposing them into new products," he says. "Whether it adds up to an economy the size of the one we have today, I doubt it," he continues, adding, with a wry smile: "I mean, I don't see a lot of billion-dollar IPOs coming out of the drive towards a lower-consuming society." But that's kind of the point. "It would be a problem if it generated as much wealth—because ultimately, the reason we feel we need to be awash in wealth is to consume. Otherwise, what's it for?"

Although MacKinnon imagines most of us will still be employed in the cash economy, in the new world order the hours will be shorter and the work often more satisfying because we'll be "participating in the production of higher-quality goods." With a smaller pot of jobs and money, some people will choose not to work and governments will provide universal basic income and/or services. Although MacKinnon avoids referencing specific anti-capitalist political systems, when pushed he agrees it looks like socialism—although "there's probably all kinds of different ways you can organise society around principles of lower consumption, none of which I think necessarily exists right now."

Most importantly, being freed from the corporate rat-race means our work-life balance shifts. We compare ourselves less to others and have more time away from screens. This change, rather than concern for the environment ("'Saving the planet' has always been a bit abstract"), is what he thinks will be most compelling to most people. We participate in communal activities, such as tending public gardens, engage in social movements and take care of children and elders. "It's the balance most of us seem to want, right? More time to engage with friends and family and to have long conversations. There are lots of opportunities, I think, for people to genuinely feel they have a higher quality of life."

Over the decades various communities have practised "voluntary simplicity," whether by choice or necessity. For the book, MacKinnon visited, among other places, sleepy Sado Island in the Sea of Japan; a farming community outside Tokyo; and the suburbs of Seattle where, since the 1990s, many folks have embraced "downshifting" in reaction to the city's conquest by the moneyed tech crowd (the most widespread rejection of consumer culture in recent times).

In general, these people buy few clothes, read library books, walk or catch buses, avoid social media and rarely listen to music or watch TV. When I ask MacKinnon whether he noticed anything distinctive about them his face lights up. "Talking to somebody working in corporate America versus somebody who's been practising voluntary simplicity for three decades is night and day, in terms of the kind of human being they are. It makes you want to be the voluntary simplicity person very much," he says. "They make time for people and have more depth and generosity of spirit. At times, it did feel like I was talking to a more evolved being."

Such lifestyles sound very worthy, I say, but also a tad… unfun? Needless to say, I am not an evolved being and I cringe as I realise how shallow I sound. Yet in my former job as a fashion editor, I have seen consumerism at its most seductive. And the first place I visited once lockdown lifted was Selfridges—possibly London's shiniest temple to materialism—to marvel at the displays. It's undeniable that consumerism brings bright lights, dazzling outfits and lively nights out.

MacKinnon gamely fields the query. "I think there's a grain of truth in it," he says. "That's the reality we need to confront, to some extent. We're certainly not talking about a return to the Stone Age, but maybe we have to accept that a lower-consuming society isn't an endless parade of distractions like the society we have today."

Getting people to believe that this can be a satisfying existence will be the biggest hurdle. "When what you've known throughout your lifetime is what satisfaction you can draw from a consumeristic materialistic society, it's very hard to imagine there's an alternative that's going to work as well or better," he says. "But there is."

He points to an uplifting case study from London. In Barking and Dagenham, one of the city's poorest boroughs, the "Every One. Every Day" initiative brings together locals to cook, partake in poetry, craft and hair-braiding sessions, and spruce up common areas, all of it free. "For many of the people participating, it's deeply engaging and profoundly affecting," he says. "In a lot of places, if you don't have the cash to consume, there's nothing to do; the closest I came to tears in researching this book was watching people who were feeling isolated and excluded from consumer culture have an alternative put in front of them. That points towards the potential."

Although a "cloak-and-dagger" culture still enshrouds talk about reducing consumption in most corporate environments—various interviewees would only speak to MacKinnon anonymously—there are some promising signs. Trailblazing brands such as Patagonia and Levi's have made impressive strides in encouraging customers to question throwaway culture and "buy less but better" is becoming a more common refrain in parts of the fashion industry (even as the industry continues to grow exponentially).

Perhaps the book's most startling comment comes from Abdullah al Maher, the CEO of a Bangladesh knitwear firm that produces for fast-fashion giants including H&M and Zara. He admits that transitioning to a lower-consuming society would be painful for his country: its 6,000 clothing factories would probably halve. But in this new system, the factories would provide better wages, pollute less and compete on quality instead of speed. "There'll be no ratrace then," Maher says, adding: "You know, it wouldn't be so bad."

It's a striking statement from a powerful businessman in a nation that is a factory for the world. And it's the sort of comment that gives MacKinnon confidence. "I'm hopeful that, coming out of the pandemic, people are going to have discussions that start to move the idea of reducing consumption back into the public discourse, from the fringes where it's been for three decades," he says.

Such conversations will involve tossing up whether we're prepared to give up our vibrant, high-velocity, acquisitive lives in order to calm our minds and save the earth. Although we might not like the answer, and change is always uncomfortable, it's tough to argue that there's even a contest.

Viewpoint 2

> *"Second-hand markets may counteract the tendencies of the throwaway society ... and can demonstrate successful examples of a circular economy. Nonetheless, engaging in second-hand shopping channels is not as straightforward as first-cycle retail."*

A Circular Economy Is Not Easy to Implement

Lea Becker Frahm, Casper Boks, and Linda Nhu Laursen

Many societies today have a linear economy: An item is bought, used, and then thrown away, to be taken to a landfill. Increasingly, experts are calling for a change to a circular economy: An item is bought, used, and then reused. It may be given away, resold, or repurposed, depending on the item and its condition. In this viewpoint, the study authors examine the incentives consumers have to participate in a circular economy as well as the barriers that exist in our current linear economy. Lea Becker Frahm and Linda Nhu Laursen are part of the technical faculty of IT and Design, Department of Architecture, Design, and Media Technology, Aalborg University (AAU), Denmark. Casper Boks is part of the faculty of Architecture and Design, Department of Design, Norwegian University of Science and Technology (NTNU), Norway.

As you read, consider the following questions:

1. Why are consumer attitudes important when it comes to changing the economy?
2. Do some forms of circular economy have fewer barriers than others?
3. What are some ways you can participate in the circular economy?

Introduction

Consumers' attitude plays a critical role in the successful implementation of a circular economy. Since 2015, there has been a growing interest in research about designing products and services for a circular economy, especially with a focus on circular production methods [1,2,3]. However, several scholars emphasise the importance of understanding user behaviour and motivation in the context of circular value offerings to ensure their acceptance and willingness to partake [4,5,6,7,8]. Without the consumers' acceptance, a circular economy will hardly last.

Circular economy comes in many forms and may be defined as a: "regenerative system in which resource input and waste, emission, and energy leakage are minimised by slowing, closing, and narrowing material and energy loops." [9]. Hence, some ways to attain a circular economy is by passing on products as heirlooms [10,11,12], physical or online reselling (second-hand) shops [13,14,15,16,17,18,19], peer-to-peer (P2P) sharing/renting platforms [20, 21], refurbishing [22,23,24], etc. In short, the common goal of circular economies is to slow and close consumption loops [25].

Second-hand markets play an important role in realising a circular economy. Gregson and Crewe [16, 26] argue that second-hand shopping channels demonstrate consumers' willingness to purchase second-hand goods and that usability continues beyond the first cycle. This is furthermore supported by the fact that second-hand markets have grown remarkably and reached a value of 96 billion dollars in 2021 [27,28,29]. Second-hand markets may counteract the tendencies of the throwaway society [30] and can demonstrate successful examples of a circular economy. Nonetheless, engaging in second-hand shopping channels is not as straightforward as first-cycle retail. Second-hand product consumption requires expertise and knowledge on how to act in unpredictable situations [31,32,33]. Many rules are unspoken: In some second-hand shopping channels haggling is acceptable and almost expected, while others do not appreciate it [15, 16, 34]. Similarly, some shops encourage consumers to rummage and partake in revalorising the products. In contrast, other shops aspire to a gallery-like atmosphere, where products are to be admired at a distance [16, 35, 36]. Hence, shopping for second-hand items requires adaptability and a willingness to take risks, which may appeal to some shoppers but deter others.

Current research offers a vast but divided stream of literature on consumers' barriers and motivations for second-hand product consumption. Some focus on only the motivational factors (e.g., motivation to purchase vintage vs. second-hand fashion [37], and critical, economic and recreational drivers [38]), while others also include barriers (e.g., the general attitude towards alternative consumption models [39], consumers barriers and motivations to second-hand product consumption [40], and perceived risk and value in second-hand clothing consumption [41]). The barriers and motivations are often connected with a single overall product category, such as clothing in [20, 37, 41, 42] or consumer segments (e.g., women vs. men [43], Child-Item Shoppers, Retailers, Habituals, Economic Transition Shoppers, Movers, Specific-Needs Shoppers, Collectors, Social Buyers, Bargain-Hunters/Browsers/Bored, and Obligees [44], Thrift-seekers vs. Creativists [45], consignment store shoppers vs. thrift store shoppers vs. online store shoppers [46]). Hence, the current literature appears fragmented, and as a result, it is difficult to get an overview of barriers and motivations for second-hand product shopping. Therefore, this study aims to bring together the streams of literature and, through empirical studies, answer the research question:

What are the barriers and motivations for second-hand product consumption, and how are these intertwined?

Theory

In the vast stream of literature on second-hand product consumption, many terms are used to describe shopping channels for selling pre-used products. Some known terms are garage sales [44, 47], thrift shops [45, 48,49,50,51], non-profit charity shops [15, 16, 36, 40, 52], car-boot sales [16, 31], nearly new sales [53, 54], flea markets [55], retro shops [56, 57], vintage shops [37, 58], etc. In this study, second-hand shop/shopping channel is used as a blanket term for all shopping channels (brick-and-mortar and online) that facilitate the resell of unspecified pre-used products.

As the purpose of this study is to investigate how barriers and motivations to second-hand product consumption are intertwined and affected by different factors, the researchers argue that a general and broad perspective is required to create an initial overview, which can lay the foundation for further studies into specific barriers, motivations, contexts, product categories, etc. The following reviews the barriers and motivations for second-hand product consumption described in prior studies.

Barriers to Second-hand Product Consumption

In this study, barriers to second-hand product consumption are factors that deter or prevent individuals from purchasing and using pre-owned items. These barriers can be categorized into several broad areas:

Certain individuals encounter social unacceptability and stigma within their social circles when engaging in second-hand product consumption, as highlighted in several studies [41, 59,60,61,62,63,64]. On the financial front, some perceive second-hand product consumption as risky due to the absence of warranty [22, 65]. In contrast, others find the effort required to purchase second-hand products outweighs the minimal monetary savings [22, 66]. The desire for new products, such as the attraction to the scent of a new car, remains a persistent barrier for some, who prefer being the first owner [39].

Fear of contamination is a widely explored aspect, containing several parameters. The hygiene concerns often manifest as fear or disgust related to potential pathogens from previous owners [67,68,69,70,71]. Research indicates that this fear is more pronounced with items closely associated with the body, such as clothing or watches [22, 39]. Similarly, concerns about pests is often linked to textile products, where consumers worry about bringing home bugs or pests [39]. While some contamination concerns may be rooted in imagination, physical and digital marks on products, decreasing their functional value, are noted, termed as 'negative utility' by Baxter et al. [67, 68]. The rejection of second-hand items due to expected technological obsolescence is also observed [22]. The concept of 'negative territory' encompassing the rejection of pre-used products based on unwanted previous users or environments, is associated with factors such as marks and smells [41, 67, 68]. However, studies show consumers with prior experience in second-hand product consumption exhibit fewer hygiene concerns compared to non-participants [69].

Historically, there has been a negative perception of second-hand shopping experience. It may be characterized by foul smells [40, 48, 72], dirty goods, and messy shops [16, 28, 35]. However, contradicting studies noted a decreasing trend in this perception [72]. Also, the irregularity and inconsistent product information in second-hand shopping channels may be frustrating for some customers [38, 73], who perceive the process of second-hand shopping as too time-consuming or thinks the location of shops is inconvenient [40, 41]. To enhance the appeal of second-hand clothing, consumers have expressed the need for improved window displays and merchandising strategies [41].

Motivations for Second-hand Product Consumption

In this study, motivations for second-hand product consumption are the factors that drive individuals to purchase and use pre-owned items. These motivations can be categorized into several key areas:

Some includes the desire to enhance their personal image by seeking originality and uniqueness [37, 38, 42, 45, 49, 74, 75]. Steward's [45] examination of two distinct groups of second-hand shoppers, namely the 'thrift-seekers' and 'creativists', reveals that the latter use second-hand shopping channels to cultivate their personal style, often driven by a sense of fun [76]. In contrast, thrift-seekers have limited financial resources, hence are motivated by frugality and seeking to maximize their purchases for the same amount of money [17, 19, 38, 39, 45, 46, 49, 74, 77,78,79,80].

Research indicates that sustainability and supporting 'the greater good' drive some individuals to opt for second-hand purchases. These ethical and ecological considerations also drive individuals to prevent waste and maintain functional products, aligning with a less wasteful lifestyle [38, 39, 49, 51, 63, 69, 81,82,83,84,85]. However, conflicting findings suggest that sustainability may play only a minor role in consumer decision-making, with motivations instead rooted in distancing from the mainstream system, using second-hand product consumption to 'escape' or 'punish' first-cycle shopping channels [38, 77].

Interestingly, contamination also can be perceived positively. Positive utility is associated with 'breaking in' products, where functional quality improves with use, as seen in leather products that initially feel too stiff. Also, positive territory, pertains to products becoming attractive based on the previous owner or their association with a relative or celebrity [67]. Acceptance of second-hand products can also stem from an appreciation for craftsmanship and the expected quality of older items, such as carpenter furniture compared to mass-produced alternatives [39, 66].

Some consumers view second-hand shopping as a 'treasure hunt,' 'bargain hunt,' or a game, finding pleasure in exploring the diverse product offerings of second-hand shopping channels [37, 38, 45, 49, 77, 80, 86]. The thrill of discovering the unexpected is a source of enjoyment for shoppers [31]. Nostalgic pleasure is another notable motivation, with some consumers seeking second-hand items as a way to connect with the past or relive personal memories [16, 37, 38, 84, 86,87,88,89,90]. This nostalgic inclination can be either historical, longing for a time not necessarily experienced, or personal, rooted in individual memories [91, 92]. Additionally, some individuals engage in second-hand shopping as a social activity, finding pleasure in spending time with family and friends or enjoying conversations with strangers they encounter during the shopping experience [38, 40].

...

Barriers

Among a group of informants, identity discrepancy was a prominent barrier. For example, a frequent answer to the question: "would you call yourself a second-hand shopper?" was that they do, in fact, shop products second-hand, but only very limited or specific product categories, and hence they do not identify as second-hand shoppers. Some explain that they find the term 'second-hand shopper' related to certain product categories or a style which they do not identify with. One informant explains that even though all his furniture (excl., the bed) is bought second-hand, he distances himself from the label 'second-hand shopper': "I'm just not a second-hand shopper. I think it comes with a certain look. I would never buy my clothes second-hand. I feel like that's what second-hand shoppers do."– Informant #7.

To some informants, the lack of exchange services is a barrier that causes them to think more thoroughly before purchasing. This was frequently mentioned as the reason for not buying gifts second-hand. One informant reports she would like the possibility to return products that did not live up to her expectations or were broken: "I wish I could return items, that did not live up to the expectations. E.g., clothes with holes. I have come home with stuff like that too many times. It's a waste of money."– Informant #5. Another says that she hardly ever purchases second-hand for her daughters anymore, as they have their own opinion on what to wear; even though a second-hand dress might be cheap, it becomes a waste of money with time.

Motivations

A few informants mentioned supporting charity as a motivation, which made them more likely to make 'risky' purchases; they argue if they do not end up using the product, they can re-donate it, and the price paid becomes some donation. Other studies found charity matters very little when shopping second-hand [15]. One informant says she considers second-hand product consumption complicated but has few exceptions: "I have bought wine glasses in charity shops sometimes when I needed some for a larger party, and then I donate them again afterwards to a specific charity shop."– Informant #19. She argues that it is cheaper than renting and that it is essential to her that it gets donated to charity organizations, which she finds particularly important.

Some seek second-hand products due to their material value (gold, leather, silk, etc.), as the value extends beyond e.g., the brand value. The informants become 'amateur experts' in seeing the difference between artificial and real leather, memorizing jewellery hallmarks, etc. They are thrilled by the hunt for (objectively) valuable items and seek second-hand markets, where the retailers usually have less knowledge about the economic value of the items for sale. "I buy all the gold jewellery I find, even if it does not fit or I don't like the design. I keep it until I have enough to melt it into a new piece of jewellery"– Informant #13.

A few informants explain how they advertise second-hand product consumption to show others what 'great things you can get' and how they like showing off their own expertise when they have found something they find valuable. Exemplified: "If people compliment something I bought second-hand, a jacket, for instance, I always say: 'Thanks, it was 250dkk in a charity shop.' I want to advertise second-hand."– Informant #13. During many of the interviews, the informants started bragging about their greatest second-hand findings.

Some informants showed considerations regarding the resell value or price of a second-hand item before purchasing: "I thought to myself that if I buy some pre-used Wegner chairs instead of new IKEA, I can always sell them if I don't want them anymore. They remain valuable, while IKEA just decreases"– Informant #9. These informants explained that they saw purchases of, e.g., designer furniture more like renting and did not expect themselves to be the last owner of the products. Hence, economically speaking, they only (expect to) invest once and purchase the replacement product with money from selling the product they already have.

The wear-and-tear of products can be positive, as consumers are less afraid of breaking them and thus feel an easier ownership. Some also prefer second-hand products with some wear-and-tear for certain occasions, e.g., parties where there is a chance a glass breaking or wine being spilt on the tablecloth: "For the last new year, I bought six wine glasses in a charity shop. I have some, but I'm too afraid they will break or that someone puts them in the dishwasher, which they cannot withstand. Then I don't have to worry."– Informant #20.

Beyond being a social activity, second-hand product consumption (in physical and online shopping channels) has also been found to be self-care, a recreational activity. The informants tell how they enjoy browsing second-hand shops all alone to spend quality time with themselves. While explaining this during the interviews, the informants did not talk about specific products or shops but focused on elaborating on what sounded like an almost meditative process of systematically looking through the products: "I can spend hours in second-hand shops alone! Just starting at one end and finishing at the other. It's balm to the soul."– Informant #14. Other informants tell how they scroll through online second-hand platforms as a substitute for social media.

...

Conclusion

This study contributes to developing and extending existing literature by defining and nuance barriers and motivations to second-hand product consumption. The research summarises barriers and motivations to second-hand product consumption and extends existing knowledge by defining two additional barriers (identity discrepancy and lack of exchange service) and six motivations (supporting charity, material value, showing off expertise, resale value, easy ownership, and self-care). Furthermore, four deviant cases of complex and intertwined barriers and motivations for second-hand product consumption are analysed and discussed, resulting in four key insights:

1) *The barriers and motivations to second-hand product consumption depend on context, shopping experience, and owner vs. buyer relation:* While prior studies investigate second-hand product consumers as people to which a single set of barriers and motivations apply (e.g [45, 46]), this study reveals a dichotomy in the attitudes of young parents towards second-hand products, with a strong inclination towards purchasing pre-used items for their children but opting for new garments for themselves. There is a notable acceptance of second-hand items for children, attributed to cost-effectiveness, social norms, and the convenient shopping experience provided by dedicated second-hand stores for children's items. However, the same informants decline to purchase second-hand products for themselves due

to time consumption, social stigma, and inconvenient shopping experiences. These findings suggest future research needs to examine consumer segments with a finer granularity, focusing on behaviour within different contexts.

2) *The undesirable shopping experiences in second-hand shopping channels overrule the intentions and desires of more sustainable consumption behaviours:* Consumers who are interested in buying more second-hand products and have no issues with, e.g., hygiene barriers, still do not purchase these products due to undesirable shopping experiences in second-hand shopping channels. This is because the process is often too time-consuming, the shops are disorganised, and the product information is inconsistent or unavailable. As a result, it is difficult to find precisely what you are looking for, and this overrules the intentions and desires of more sustainable consumption behaviours (intention-behaviour gap). Hence, research on barriers and motivations to second-hand product consumption related to the shopping experience must be further developed or implemented in praxis. This finding adds nuances to the ongoing discussion on whether sustainable consumption is the main driver for second-hand product consumption [39, 49, 63] or not [38, 77].

3) *Treasure hunting is just as much about the hunt as it is about second-hand treasures:* The study highlights second-hand shopping as akin to a treasure hunt, a distinct experience many informants cherish, which extends several prior studies that emphasise treasure hunting as a solid motivation for second-hand product consumption (e.g [38, 80]). This unique aspect, vital for their engagement, warrants further investigation. The specific parameters shaping this experience, such as the thrill of discovery and the satisfaction of looking (but not necessarily finding) bargains, should be better defined in future research, or applied in practice to enhance consumer engagement with second-hand shopping channels. Understanding and harnessing

the allure of treasure hunting could optimise strategies for sustainable consumption.

4) *The barriers and motivations to second-hand product consumption depend more on the specific product type than the product category:* The analysis emphasises that barriers and motivations to second-hand product consumption are intricately tied to particular product types rather than broad product categories, such as many previous studies have tackled it (e.g [41, 42, 59, 83]). Hygiene concerns vary significantly depending on the nature of the product – for instance, informants exhibit reluctance towards purchasing second-hand underwear but are comfortable with pre-owned swimwear. This distinction suggests that the decision-making process regarding second-hand items is more finely tuned to the product's specific context and usage rather than solely based on its overarching category, which goes in line with prior studies of barriers and motivations to purchasing refurbished products [22]. Hence, future studies must look more closely at product types rather than categories.

...

References

1. Boks C (2018) An introduction to design for sustainable behaviour. In: Egenhoefer RB (ed) Routledge handbook of sustainable design, Book, Section bd., Red., Routledge, s. 315–327. https://www.taylorfrancis.com/chapters/edit/10.4324/9781315625508-28/introduction-design-sustainable-behaviour-casper-boks
2. Camacho-Otero J, Boks C, Pettersen IN (2018) Consumption in the circular economy: a literature review. Sustainability 10(8):2758
3. van Dam K, Simeone L, Keskin D, Baldassarre B, Niero M, Morelli N (2020) Circular economy in industrial design research: a review. Sustainability 12(24):10279
4. Ackermann L (2018) Design for product care: enhancing consumers' repair and maintenance activities. Des J 21(4):543–551
5. Bhamra T, Lilley D, Tang T (2011) Design for sustainable behaviour: Using products to change consumer behaviour. Des J 14(4):427–445
6. Daae J, Chamberlin L, Boks C (2018) Dimensions of behaviour change in the context of designing for a circular economy. Des J 21(4):521–541
7. Hobson K, Lynch N (2016) Diversifying and de-growing the circular economy: radical social transformation in a resource-scarce world. Futures 82(Journal Article):15–25
8. Jackson T (2005) Motivating sustainable consumption. Sustain Dev Res Netw 29(1):30–40

9. Geissdoerfer M, Savaget P, Bocken NM, Hultink EJ (2017) The circular economy–a new sustainability paradigm? J Clean Prod 143(Journal Article):757–768
10. Frahm LB, Laursen LN, Tollestrup C (2022) Categories and design properties of inherited long-lasting products. Sustainability 14(7):3835
11. Price LL, Arnould EJ, Folkman Curasi C (2000) Older consumers' disposition of special possessions. J Consum Res 27(2):179–201
12. Wells VK, Carrigan M, Athwal N (2023) Holding on or letting go: Inheritance as a liminal experience. Mark Theory 23(3):509–532
13. Appelgren S, Bohlin A (2015) Growing in motion: the circulation of used things on second-hand markets. Cult Unbound 7(1):143–168
14. Bohlin A (2019) It will keep circulating': loving and letting go of things in Swedish second-hand markets. Worldw Waste J Interdiscip Stud 2(1). https://doi.org/10.5334/wwwj.17
15. Gregson N, Crewe L, Brooks K (2002) Shopping, space, and practice. Environ Plan Soc Space 20(5):597–617
16. Gregson N, Crewe ogL (2003) Second-hand cultures. Materializing culture. Berg, Oxford. doi: https://doi.org/10.2752/9781847888853.
17. Park H, Joyner Armstrong CM (2019) Is money the biggest driver? Uncovering motives for engaging in online collaborative consumption retail models for apparel. J Retail Consum Serv 51:42–50. https://doi.org/10.1016/j.jretconser.2019.05.022
18. Rahman SU, Makkonen H (2022) Is this a new era for old goods? Analysing the motives for second-hand product resale in the platform economy. Int J Export Mark 5(3–4):296–319. https://doi.org/10.1504/IJEXPORTM.2022.130498
19. Saarijärvi H, Joensuu J, Rintamaki T, Yrjölä M (2018) One person's trash is another person's treasure: Profiling consumer-to-consumer e-commerce in Facebook. Int J Retail Distrib Manag 46(11/12):1092–1107. https://doi.org/10.1108/IJRDM-04-2017-0091
20. Ek M, Styvén MM, Mariani (2020) Understanding the intention to buy secondhand clothing on sharing economy platforms: The influence of sustainability, distance from the consumption system, and economic motivations. Psychol Mark 37(5):724–739. https://doi.org/10.1002/mar.21334
21. Parguel B, Lunardo R, Benoit-Moreau F (2017) Sustainability of the sharing economy in question: When second-hand peer-to-peer platforms stimulate indulgent consumption. Technol Forecast Soc Change 125(Journal Article):48–57
22. Mugge R, Safari I, Balkenende R (2017) Is there a market for refurbished toothbrushes? An exploratory study on consumers' acceptance of refurbishment for different product categories. PLATE Prod Lifetimes Environ (Journal Article):293–297 https://doi.org/10.3233/978-1-61499-820-4-293
23. Mugge R, de Jong W, Person O, Hultink EJ (2018) If It Ain't Broke, Don't Explain It': the influence of visual and verbal information about prior use on consumers' evaluations of refurbished electronics. Des J 21(4):499–520
24. van Weelden E, Mugge R, Bakker C (2016) Paving the way towards circular consumption: exploring consumer acceptance of refurbished mobile phones in the Dutch market. J Clean Prod 113:743–754. https://doi.org/10.1016/j.jclepro.2015.11.065
25. Ellen MacArthur Foundation (2013) Towards the circular economy. J Ind Ecol 2(1):23–44
26. Gregson N, Crewe L (1994) Beyond the high street and the mall: car boot fairs and the new geographies of consumption in the 1990s. Area (Journal Article):261–267. https://www.jstor.org/stable/20003456

27. Kim S, Woo H (2021) Big data analysis of trends in the second-hand apparel market: a comparison between 2014 and 2019. Res J Text Appar 26(2):138–155. https://doi.org/10.1108/RJTA-12-2020-0139
28. Ross GR, Bolton LE, Meloy MG (2023) Disorder in secondhand retail spaces: The countervailing forces of hidden treasure and risk. J Retail 99(1):136–148. https://doi.org/10.1016/j.jretai.2022.12.002
29. Thredup (2024) Secondhand apparel market value worldwide from 2021 to 2028 (in billion U.S. dollars) [Graph]. In: Statista. Retrieved September 16, 2024, from https://www.statista.com/statistics/826162/apparel-resale-market-value-worldwide/
30. Cooper T (2005) Slower consumption reflections on product life spans and the 'throwaway society'. J Ind Ecol 9(1–2):51–67
31. Crewe L, Gregson N (1998) Tales of the unexpected: exploring car boot sales as marginal spaces of contemporary consumption. Trans Inst Br Geogr 23(1):39–53
32. Gregson N (1997) Crewe L (1997) The bargain, the knowledge, and the spectacle: making sense of consumption in the space of the car-boot sale - Nicky Gregson, Louise Crewe. Environ Plan Soc Space 15(1):87–112. https://doi.org/10.1068/d150087
33. Parsons E (2005) Dealing in secondhand goods: creating meaning and value. In: Ekstrom KM, Brembeck H (eds) E - European advances in consumer research, vol 7. Association for Consumer Research, Goteborg, pp 189–194. https://acrwebsite.org/volumes/13770/eacr/vol7/E-07
34. Herrmann GM (2004) Haggling spoken here: gender, class, and style in US garage sale bargaining. J Pop Cult 38(1):55
35. Frahm LB, Laursen LN, Christensen BT (2024) Creating a mess! Design strategies for managing visual complexity in second-hand shops, præsenteret ved Design Research Society, Boston, https://doi.org/10.21606/drs.2024.773
36. Frahm LB, Laursen LN, Tollestrup C (2023) Everyone does it-product-related resell strategies of professional second-hand retailers. In: PLATE-Product Lifetime And The Environment. https://aaltodoc.aalto.fi/items/b103abbc-199c-499c-8020-a2690b7cb956
37. Cervellon M, Carey L, Harms T (2012) Something old, something used: determinants of women's purchase of vintage fashion vs second-hand fashion. Int J Retail Distrib Manag 40(12):956–974
38. Guiot D, Roux D (2010) A second-hand shoppers' motivation scale: antecedents, consequences, and implications for retailers. J Retail 86(4):355–371
39. Edbring EG, Lehner M, Mont O (2016) Exploring consumer attitudes to alternative models of consumption: motivations and barriers. J Clean Prod 123(Journal Article):5–15
40. Frahm LB, Laursen LN, Boks C (2023) Smells like grandparents: consumers' barriers and motivations to second-hand shopping. præsenteret ved Product Lifetime And The Environment (PLATE), Finland
41. Hur E (2020) Rebirth fashion: secondhand clothing consumption values and perceived risks. J Clean Prod 273(Journal Article):122951
42. Jägel T, Keeling K, Reppel A, Gruber T (2012) Individual values and motivational complexities in ethical clothing consumption: a means-end approach. J Mark Manag 28(3–4):373–396
43. Gregson N, Crewe L (1998) Dusting down second hand rose: Gendered identities and the world of second-hand goods in the space of the car boot sale. Gend Place Cult 5(1):77–100. https://doi.org/10.1080/09663699825331

44. Herrmann GM, Soiffer SM (1984) For fun and profit: An analysis of the American garage sale. Urban Life 12(4):397–421
45. Steward S (2020) What does that shirt mean to you? Thrift-store consumption as cultural capital. J Consum Cult 20(4):457–477
46. Zaman M, Park H, Kim Y-K, Park S-H (2019) Consumer orientations of second-hand clothing shoppers. J Glob Fash Mark 10(2):163–176\
47. Parrish R (1986) A garage-sale is never as simple as youd think, theres always something that, stays to haunt you, especially if youre a stubborn bargainer an experience in Switzerland. Smithsonian 17(9):133
48. Bardhi F (2003) Thrill of the hunt: thrift shopping for pleasure. Adv Consum Res 30(Journal Article):375–376
49. Bardhi F, Arnould EJ (2005) Thrift shopping: Combining utilitarian thrift and hedonic treat benefits. J Consum Behav Int Res Rev 4(4):223–233
50. Larsen F (2023) Selling thrift: work practices in an American thrift store. J Bus Anthropol 12(1):1. https://doi.org/10.22439/jba.v12i1.6914
51. Park H, Kwon TA, Zaman MM, Song SY (2020) Thrift shopping for clothes: To treat self or others? J Glob Fash Mark 11(1):56–70. https://doi.org/10.1080/20932685.2019.1684831
52. Parsons E (2002) People or profits? The challenges of managing in charity retail. Institute for Retail Studies, University of Stirling.
53. Clarke A (2000) Mother swapping: the trafficking of nearly new children's wear. In: Jackson P, Lowe M, Miller D, Mort F (eds) Commercial cultures: economies, practices, spaces. Berg, Oxford, pp 85–100
54. Waight E (2015) Buying for baby: how middle-class mothers negotiate risk with second-hand goods. Intimacies Crit Consum Diverse Econ (Journal Article):197–215
55. Belk RW, Sherry JF Jr, Wallendorf M (1988) A naturalistic inquiry into buyer and seller behavior at a swap meet. J Consum Res 14(4):449–470
56. Baker SE (2012) Retailing retro: class, cultural capital and the material practices of the (re) valuation of style. Eur J Cult Stud 15(5):621–641
57. Crewe L, Gregson N, Brooks K (2003) The Discursivities of Difference: Retro retailers and the ambiguities of 'the alternative'. J Consum Cult 3(1):61–82. https://doi.org/10.1177/1469540503003001931
58. Knowles K (2024) Locating vintage, 2015, Set: 21. [Online]. Tilgængelig hos: https://www.necsus-ejms.org/test/locating-vintage/
59. Armstrong CM, Niinimäki K, Kujala S, Karell E, Lang C (2015) Sustainable product-service systems for clothing: exploring consumer perceptions of consumption alternatives in Finland. J Clean Prod 97(Journal Article):30–39. https://doi.org/10.1016/j.jclepro.2014.01.046
60. Habinc M (2018) Second-hand clothes shops in Slovenia: the contemporary situation in its (A) historical perspective. Stud Ethnol Croat (30):321–343. https://doi.org/10.17234/SEC.30.1
61. Kim I, Jung HJ, Lee Y (2021) Consumers' value and risk perceptions of circular fashion: Comparison between secondhand, upcycled, and recycled clothing. Sustainability 13(3):1208
62. Lang og C, Zhang R (2019) Second-hand clothing acquisition: the motivations and barriers to clothing swaps for Chinese consumers. Sustain Prod Consum 18(Journal Article):156–164. https://doi.org/10.1016/j.spc.2019.02.002
63. Sandes FS, Leandro J (2019) Exploring the motivations and, barriers for second, hand product consumption. Glob Fash Manag Conf 2019(Journal Article):292–296. https://doi.org/10.15444/GFMC2019.02.08.05

64. Valor C, Ronda L, Abril C (2022) Understanding the expansion of circular markets: Building relational legitimacy to overcome the stigma of second-hand clothing. Sustain Prod Consum 30(Journal Article):77–88
65. Kaplan M, Gültekin Y (2024) A review of factors affecting the behavior of purchasing second-hand products from C2C online platforms. In: International Research in Social, Human and Administrative Sciences XVII, 1. udg., Eğitim Yayinevi, s. 7–19. https://avesis.comu.edu.tr/yayin/970930aa-d545-4d99-b11a-9e973c7ea7cd/a-review-of-factors-affecting-the-behavior-of-purchasing-second-hand-products-from-c2c-online-platforms
66. Henseling C, Blättel-Mink B, Clausen J, Erdmann L (2010) Contribution of online trading of used goods to resource efficiency: an empirical study of eBay users. Sustainability 2(6):1810–1830. https://doi.org/10.3390/su2061810
67. Baxter W, Aurisicchio M, Mugge R, Childs P (2017) Positive and negative contamination in user interactions, præsenteret ved DS 87– 8 Proceedings of the 21st International Conference on Engineering Design (ICED 17) Vol 8: Human Behaviour in Design, Vancouver, Canada, 21-25.08. 2017, s. 509–518
68. Baxter WL, Aurisicchio M, Childs PR (2016) Materials, use and contaminated interaction. Mater Des 90(Journal Article):1218–1227
69. Silva SC, Santos A, Duarte P, Vlačić B (2021) The role of social embarrassment, sustainability, familiarity and perception of hygiene in second-hand clothing purchase experience. Int J Retail Distrib Manag 49(6):717–734
70. Wallner TS, Magnier L, Mugge R (2022) Do consumers mind contamination by previous users? A choice-based conjoint analysis to explore strategies that improve consumers' choice for refurbished products. Resour Conserv Recycl 177(Journal Article):105998
71. Wallner TS, Snel S, Magnier L, Mugge R (2022) Contaminated by its prior use: strategies to design and market refurbished personal care products. Circ Econ Sust 3:1077–1098. https://doi.org/10.1007/s43615-022-00197-3
72. Mitchell M, Montgomery R (2010) An examination of thrift store shoppers. Mark Manag J 20(2):94–107
73. Akerlof GA (1978) The market for 'lemons': quality uncertainty and the market mechanism. In: Uncertainty in economics, Book, Section bd., Elsevier, s. 235–251. https://doi.org/10.1016/B978-0-12-214850-7.50022-X
74. Herjanto H, Scheller-Sampson J, Erickson E (2016) The increasing phenomenon of second-hand clothes (2016) Purchase: insights from the literature. J Manaj Dan Wirausaha 18(1):1–15. https://doi.org/10.9744/jmk.18.1.1-15
75. Tian KT, Bearden WO, Hunter GL (2001) Consumers' need for uniqueness: scale development and validation. J Consum Res 28(1):50–66. https://doi.org/10.1086/321947
76. Kessous A, Valette-Florence P (2019) 'From Prada to Nada': consumers and their luxury products: a contrast between second-hand and first-hand luxury products. J Bus Res 102:313–327. https://doi.org/10.1016/j.jbusres.2019.02.033
77. Ferraro C, Sands S, Brace-Govan J (2016) The role of fashionability in second-hand shopping motivations. J Retail Consum Serv 32(Journal Article):262–268
78. James S, Brown RB, Goodsell TL, Stovall J, Flaherty J (2010) Adapting to hard times: Family participation patterns in local thrift economies. Fam Relat 59(4):383–395
79. Kasser T (2011) Can thrift bring well-being? A review of the research and a tentative theory. Soc Personal Psychol Compass 5(11):865–877
80. Silva SC, Duarte P, Sandes FS, Almeida CA (2022) The hunt for treasures, bargains and individuality in pre-loved luxury. Int J Retail Distrib Manag 50(11):1321–1336. https://doi.org/10.1108/IJRDM-10-2021-0466

81. Borusiak B, Szymkowiak A, Horska E, Raszka N, Żelichowska E (2020) Towards building sustainable consumption: A study of second-hand buying intentions. Sustainability 12(3):875
82. Franklin A (2011) The ethics of second-hand consumption. In: Ethical consumption: a critical introduction. Routledge. https://www.routledge.com/Ethical-Consumption-A-Critical-Introduction/Lewis-Potter/p/book/9780415558259
83. Niinimäki K (2010) Eco-clothing, consumer identity and ideology. Sustain Dev 18(3):150–162
84. Sihvonen J, Turunen LLM (2016) As good as new– valuing fashion brands in the online second-hand markets. J Prod Brand Manag 25(3):285–295. https://doi.org/10.1108/JPBM-06-2015-0894
85. Waight E (2013) Eco babies: reducing a parent's ecological footprint with second-hand consumer goods. Int J Green Econ 7(2):197–211
86. Roux D, Guiot D (2008) Measuring second-hand shopping motives, antecedents and consequences. Rech Appl En Mark Engl Ed 23(4):63–91
87. Banister EN, Hogg MK, Decrop A, Roux D (2005) Clothes make the man: symbolic consumption and second hand clothing. In: Ekstrom KM, Brembeck H (eds) E - European advances in consumer research, vol 7. Association for Consumer Research, Goteborg, pp 455–456. http://www.acrwebsite.org/volumes/13682/eacr/vol7/E-07
88. Goulding C (2002) An exploratory study of age related vicarious nostalgia and aesthetic consumption. Adv Consum Res 29(1):542–546
89. Holak SL, Havlena WJ (1992) Nostalgia: an exploratory study of themes and emotions in the nostalgic experience. Adv Consum Res 19(1)
90. Roux D (2008) Hunting around for meaning in the market: the quest for ethics and identity among buyers of secondhand goods. Haettu 19:49–70. https://www.researchgate.net/profile/Dominique-Roux-3/publication/259474893_Hunting_around_for_meaning_in_the_market_the_quest_for_ethics_and_identity_among_buyers_of_secondhand_goods/links/5791be9f08ae108aa041ba68/Hunting-around-for-meaning-in-the-market-the-quest-for-ethics-and-identity-among-buyers-of-secondhand-goods.pdf
91. Phau I, Marchegiani C (2009) Assessing varying intensities of personal nostalgia on emotions. In: Dewi T (ed) Australian and New Zealand marketing academy conference. Australian and New Zealand Marketing Academy, Melbourne. http://hdl.handle.net/20.500.11937/40664
92. Stern BB (1992) Historical and personal nostalgia in advertising text: the fin de siecle effect. J Advert 21(4):11–22
93. Dubois A, Gadde L-E (2002) Systematic combining: an abductive approach to case research. J Bus Res 55(7):553–560
94. Kvale S, Brinkmann S (2015) Interview–det kvalitative forskningsinterview som håndværk, 3. udg. Hans Reitzels Forlag, København
95. Tanggard L, Brinkmann S (2020) Interviewet: samtalen som forskningsmetode. In: Kvalitative Metoder - En grundbog, Book, Section bd., Hans Reitzels Forlag, s. 33–63
96. Hanington B, Martin B (2019) Universal methods of design: 125 ways to research complex problems, develop innovative ideas, and design effective solutions, Expanded and Revised edition. Rockport Publishers. https://www.vlebooks.com/vleweb/product/openreader?id=none&isbn=9781631597497
97. Harboe G, Huang EM (2015) Real-world affinity diagramming practices: bridging the paper-digital gap. In: Proceedings of the 33rd annual ACM conference on human

factors in computing systems, i CHI '15. Association for Computing Machinery, New York, NY, USA, apr. s. 95–104. https://doi.org/10.1145/2702123.2702561
98. Kolko J (2011) Exposing the magic of design: a practitioner's guide to the methods and theory of synthesis. I Human Technology Interaction Series, no. Book, whole. Oxford University Press, United Kingdom. https://doi.org/10.1093/acprof:oso/9780199744336.001.0001
99. Flyvbjerg B (2006) Five misunderstandings about case-study research. Qual Inq 12(2): 219–245
100. Acharya AS, Prakash A, Saxena P, Nigam A (2013) Sampling: why and how of it. Indian J Med Spec 4(2):330–333
101. Flyvbjerg B (2020) Fem misforståelser om casestudiet. In: Kvalitative Metoder - En grundbog, 3. udg., Book, Section bd., S. Brinkmann og L. Tanggaard, Red., Hans Reitzels Forlag, s. 621–651
102. Qu SQ, Dumay J (2011) The qualitative research interview. Qual Res Account. Manag 8(3):238–264. https://doi.org/10.1108/11766091111162070
103. CofieN. Braund H. Dalgarno N (2022) Eight ways to get a grip on intercoder reliability using qualitative-based measures. Can Med Educ J Rev Can Léducation Médicale 13(2):73–76, 2022. https://doi.org/10.36834/cmej.72504
104. Wang B, Fu Y, Li Y (2022) Young consumers' motivations and barriers to the purchase of second-hand clothes: an empirical study of China. Waste Manag 143(Journal Article):157–167
105. Bridgens B, Lilley D (2017) Design for next… year. The challenge of designing for material change. Des J 20(sup1):S160–S171
106. Lilley D, Smalley G, Bridgens B, Wilson GT, Balasundaram K (2016) Cosmetic obsolescence? User perceptions of new and artificially aged materials. Mater Des 101(Journal Article):355–365
107. Lilley D, Bridgens B, Davies A, Holstov A (2019) Ageing (dis) gracefully: Enabling designers to understand material change. J Clean Prod 220(Journal Article):417–430

The UN Environment Programme's (UNEP's) recent report From Pollution to Solution shows there is currently between 75-199 million tons of plastic waste in the ocean, and in 2016 some 9-14 tons of waste entered the aquatic ecosystem. It is estimated that by 2040, this will have almost tripled to 23-37 million tons per year. Plastics are the largest, most harmful and most persistent of marine litter, accounting for at least 85 per cent of all marine waste.

But experts say, simply binning SUPPs and switching to single-use products made of other materials is not the solution.

"It is the single-use nature of products that is the most problematic for the planet, more so than the material that they're made of," says Claudia Giacovelli, Programme Officer of the UNEP Life Cycle Unit. "The best solution may not be the same in all societies but taking a life cycle approach can help in setting the base towards the right decision."

So how can we phase out SUPPs and what are the alternatives?

Here are some recommendations from UNEP and the Life Cycle Initiative's meta-analyses of life cycle assessment studies on SUPPs:

Opt for reusable alternatives

Prioritizing reusable products is not only critical for environmental health, but it can also be cost-effective. Businesses that allow consumers to bring their own bags, cups or containers can save on SUPP-associated supply and storage expenditure, while customers can avoid potentially paying extra for shopping bags or containers.

Cotton and non-woven polypropylene shopping bags are increasingly common, as are reusable and portable plastic and stainless steel bottles, cups, and tableware. Reusability is also increasingly viable for personal hygiene products, through products like silicone menstrual cups and cloth nappies.

Turn 'single-use' into 'multi-use'

The more any product is reused, the lower its environmental impact. When consumers can't avoid SUPPs, they should mitigate their environmental impact by reusing them when possible instead of immediately disposing of them. For example, durable single-use plastic bags, bottles, cups, tableware, and take-away food packaging can be reused or repurposed.

Single-use alternatives made of other materials are not intrinsically better, meaning that they should be reused when possible too. Such as, a paper shopping bag may need to be used four to eight times to have a lower environmental impact than one single-use plastic bag.

Design products with circularity and end-of-life consideration

Consumers should not shoulder the entire burden of decreasing the impacts of SUPP. Guided by policymaker and retailer action, products should be designed to be both lightweight and durable to maximize reusability. Production should be sustainable, such as by using renewable energy and recycled materials.

Sourcing locally and avoiding air-freight transported goods is another way to reduce the environmental impact of products over their life cycle. Finally, end-of-life impacts must be considered, so that products can be recycled or discarded in an environmentally friendly manner when they can no longer be reused.

Geographical and social context matters

As more areas propose bans to SUPPs, policymakers must consider geographical and social contexts when identifying appropriate alternatives. Factors such as production requirements, expected use, reusability, likelihood of littering, local waste management infrastructure and education can all impact how environmentally friendly proposed alternatives are.

Shifting to reusable options and bolstering recycling and waste management infrastructure must take priority. In the interim period, areas with littering problems should avoid using lighter products because they are more likely to be littered, even though they are generally less resource-intensive to produce.

Ultimately, eliminating SUPPs is only one way to reduce environmental damage.

As Giacovelli notes, "Countries are encouraged to promote actions that lead to keeping resources at their highest value in the economy, by consuming less and replacing single-use products with fit-for-purpose reusable alternatives for a healthier planet."

"How to reduce the impacts of single-use plastic products" by UNEP, November 23, 2021.

Viewpoint 3

> *"At its core, the circular economy is a transformative concept that redefines our understanding of production and consumption."*

A Circular Economy Is Crucial to Reducing Consumption

Heinrich Böll Foundation

Although there are barriers to implementing a circular economy, many experts believe that taking on this difficult task is an important part of reducing overconsumption. Stopping production of certain items could cause a shortage, but reusing and sharing or selling items can help people reduce their consumption without feeling that pinch. In this viewpoint, the Heinrich Böll Foundation explains how a functioning circular economy can be implemented and why this is so important. The Heinrich Böll Foundation is a think tank that works to promote sustainability, green policies, and environmental protection.

As you read, consider the following questions:

1. Why is a circular economy so important?
2. How can we overcome some of the barriers to implementing this type of economy?

3. What are some examples of the three pillars of a circular economy that you can implement in your own life?

The circular economy marks a significant evolution in the global approach to production, consumption, and waste management. Diverging from the traditional linear model, which is characterized by a 'take, make, dispose' process, the circular economy is predicated on the principles of reducing waste and pollution, maintaining products and materials in use for as long as possible, and regenerating natural systems. This approach is not just about recycling; it reimagines how goods are designed, used, and reused, ensuring that they can be repurposed or recycled effectively, minimizing the environmental impact . These principles have become increasingly critical, as environmental challenges escalate. With over 2 billion tons of solid waste generated annually and an estimated 8 million metric tons of plastic entering the oceans each year, the need for a sustainable approach is clear. This model isn't just about recycling; it reimagines how goods are designed, used, and reused, ensuring that they can be repurposed or recycled effectively, minimizing environmental impact.

At the heart of the circular economy lies the commitment to use renewable resources and shift towards renewable energy sources. This is crucial in a time when the world is facing severe climate change impacts, including rising global temperatures and extreme weather events. The circular economy also emphasizes the importance of restoring natural habitats and ecosystems, alongside developing regenerative agricultural systems. These combined elements make it a holistic approach to addressing some of the most pressing environmental challenges of our time, such as climate change, resource depletion, and ecological degradation.

Understanding the circular economy is crucial in a world grappling with environmental limits and seeking sustainable economic models. This concept not only offers an alternative that can lead to more sustainable economic development but also provides a framework for individuals and organizations to rethink and redesign the future of various industries and sectors. Adopting circular economy principles can significantly contribute to addressing environmental issues, setting a course for a more sustainable and resilient future.

What is the Circular Economy?

At its core, the circular economy is a transformative concept that redefines our understanding of production and consumption. In stark contrast to the traditional linear economy, which follows a 'take, make, dispose' model, the circular economy champions a sustainable approach. It is founded on the idea that resources can be utilized more efficiently and sustainably through the principles of reduce, reuse, and recycle.

The circular economy seeks to redefine growth, focusing on positive society-wide benefits. It entails gradually decoupling economic activity from the consumption of finite resources and designing waste out of the system. Unlike the linear model, which depletes resources and often leads to the accumulation of waste, the circular economy is restorative and regenerative by design. It aims to keep products, equipment, and infrastructure in use for longer, thus improving the productivity of these resources.

This innovative economic model goes beyond simply recycling materials; it requires a systemic shift in how products are designed, marketed, and consumed. It encourages the development of new business models that create sustained economic value and build robust, resilient systems capable of withstanding environmental challenges. As such, the circular economy is not only an environmental imperative but also a strategic approach to fostering long-term economic and societal well-being.

Core Principles of the Circular Economy

The circular economy is underpinned by three core principles, commonly known as the three R's: Reduce, Reuse, and Recycle. These principles serve as the guiding framework for transforming our traditional linear economy, where goods are made, used, and disposed of, into a circular one that is restorative and regenerative by design. By integrating these principles into production and consumption processes, it becomes possible to significantly reduce waste, lower greenhouse gas emissions, and conserve natural resources. Each of these principles plays a unique but complementary role in achieving the goal of a sustainable, circular economy.

Reduce

The first principle, 'Reduce,' focuses on minimizing the consumption of resources and the generation of waste. This principle advocates for more efficient use of resources, which could involve designing products that require fewer materials or consume less energy. It also emphasizes the need to reduce the volume of waste produced. For example, a practical application of this principle is seen in the design of energy-efficient appliances that use less electricity, or in packaging products with biodegradable or minimal packaging to reduce waste.

Reuse

'Reuse' is the second fundamental principle and it centers on extending the life cycle of products and materials. By finding new uses for existing products, or repurposing materials, one can avoid the need for new resources and reduce waste. An everyday example of this principle is the refurbishing and reselling of electronics. Instead of disposing of old phones or computers, they can be refurbished and sold, giving them a second life. Similarly, fashion industries are increasingly embracing the concept of upcycling, where old garments are transformed into new clothing items or other products.

Recycle

The third principle, 'Recycle,' involves converting waste materials into new products or raw materials for use in other processes. This principle is crucial in reducing the need for virgin resources and minimizing waste going to landfills. For instance, recycling paper reduces the demand for new timber, and recycling plastic means less new plastic is produced. An everyday example of recycling in action is the conversion of used glass bottles into new glass products or using recycled plastic to create outdoor furniture or clothing fibers.

Interrelation of the Principles

These three principles are deeply interconnected and form the foundation of the circular economy. Reducing resource consumption naturally leads to less waste, supporting the reuse principle. Reuse extends the life of products and materials, delaying their entry into the recycling process. Finally, recycling turns waste into resources, thereby reducing the need for new raw materials. Together, these principles create a sustainable, closed-loop system that minimizes environmental impact and promotes resource efficiency.

In practice, these principles reinforce one another. For example, a company might design a product that uses less material (Reduce), make it easy to repair (Reuse), and ensure that at the end of its life, the materials can be effectively recycled (Recycle). By integrating all three principles, the circular economy aims to create a more sustainable and environmentally friendly system of production and consumption.

Benefits of the Circular Economy

The transition to a circular economy offers a multitude of benefits across environmental, economic, and social dimensions. It presents a sustainable alternative to the traditional linear model, promising a future where economic growth is achieved in harmony with environmental stewardship and social well-being.

Environmental Benefits

One of the most significant benefits of the circular economy is its positive impact on the environment. By adopting the principles of reduce, reuse, and recycle, the amount of waste generated can be drastically reduced. This reduction in waste not only alleviates pressure on landfills and waste management systems but also decreases pollution and greenhouse gas emissions associated with waste disposal. Moreover, the circular economy promotes the conservation of resources by keeping products and materials in use for as long as possible, thus reducing the need to extract and process raw materials. This conservation is crucial in preserving biodiversity and combating resource depletion.

The circular economy also contributes to decreasing pollution beyond just waste reduction. By encouraging the design of products that are more durable and easier to repair, it reduces the frequency with which products are discarded and replaced. This shift leads to a significant decrease in the environmental pollution associated with manufacturing new products, including reduced air and water pollution and lower carbon emissions. Additionally, by focusing on renewable resources and energy, the circular economy helps in mitigating the impact of climate change.

Economic Benefits

The economic benefits of the circular economy are equally compelling. This model can lead to substantial cost savings for both businesses and consumers. For businesses, the efficient use of materials and resources can reduce production costs. The circular economy also opens up new business opportunities and markets, particularly in the fields of recycling, refurbishing, and sustainable product design.

Another significant economic advantage is job creation. The circular economy model requires a range of new skills and roles, from repairing and refurbishing to recycling and resource management. These new roles can lead to the creation of a substantial number of jobs, contributing to economic growth and stability. Moreover, by decoupling economic growth from resource consumption, the circular economy offers a pathway to sustainable growth, ensuring long-term economic resilience.

Social Benefits

The circular economy also brings several social benefits. One key aspect is community development. Local recycling and refurbishing initiatives can strengthen community ties and foster a sense of shared responsibility for the environment. These initiatives often involve local businesses and community groups, promoting local economic development and social cohesion.

Additionally, the circular economy fosters innovation. The need for sustainable product design, efficient resource use, and effective waste management drives innovation across various sectors. This innovation can lead to the development of new technologies and business models that not only benefit the environment but also offer enhanced products and services to consumers.

Challenges and Misconceptions

A prevalent misconception about the circular economy is that it is solely about recycling. While recycling is a crucial component, the circular economy encompasses a broader range of practices like reducing resource use and extending product life spans through reuse and refurbishment. It's not just about managing waste better; it's about rethinking and redesigning the entire lifecycle of products.

Another misunderstanding is the belief that the circular economy is a cost burden to businesses. In reality, it can lead to significant cost savings and new business opportunities. The transition to a circular economy often involves initial investments and a shift in business models, but these are typically offset by long-term savings and benefits.

Finally, some people assume that the circular economy can fully replace the need for raw materials. While it greatly reduces the demand for new resources, some level of raw material extraction will likely remain necessary. The goal is to minimize this need as much as possible through efficient use and reuse of materials.

Challenges in Implementing Circular Economy Practices

One of the biggest challenges is the need for systemic change. Transitioning to a circular economy requires alterations in production processes, business models, consumer behavior, and even regulation. This shift can be complex and resource-intensive, requiring collaboration across different sectors and levels of government.

Another challenge lies in the design of products and systems. For the circular economy to be effective, products need to be designed for durability, repairability, and recyclability from the outset. This requires a significant shift in design philosophy and practice, which can be difficult to implement quickly.

The infrastructure for recycling and refurbishing also needs to be expanded and improved. Many regions lack the necessary facilities and technologies to efficiently process recycled materials or refurbish used products, making it challenging to implement circular practices on a large scale.

Lastly, consumer behavior and cultural attitudes play a significant role. Shifting consumer preferences towards more sustainable products and practices is essential but can be challenging due to entrenched habits and perceptions about the desirability of new versus reused products.

Real-World Examples

The circular economy concept has been successfully implemented in various industries, demonstrating its versatility and effectiveness. Below are a few examples from the fashion, electronics, and food industries that highlight the practical application of circular economy principles.

Fashion Industry: Sustainable and Circular Fashion

In the fashion industry, companies like Patagonia and H&M have made significant strides in implementing circular economy practices. Patagonia's Worn Wear program encourages customers to return used clothing items, which are then repaired and resold, extending the lifecycle of their products. This practice not only reduces waste but also emphasizes the value of durable and repairable clothing.

H&M, on the other hand, has implemented a garment collecting initiative where customers can return any brand of used clothing. These clothes are either resold as second-hand goods, repurposed into other products like cleaning cloths, or recycled into textile fibers for new products. This approach helps in reducing the environmental impact of clothing waste and promotes sustainable fashion.

Electronics Industry: E-Waste Recycling and Refurbishment

In the electronics industry, companies like Apple and Dell have adopted circular economy practices to address the issue of e-waste. Apple has developed a robot named Daisy, which can disassemble iPhones to recover valuable materials that can be recycled. This process helps in reducing the need for mining new resources and minimizes waste.

Dell has implemented a closed-loop recycling system where it recycles plastics from old computers into new ones. This system reduces the need for new plastic production, thereby conserving resources and reducing environmental impact.

Food Industry: Sustainable Packaging and Waste Reduction

In the food industry, initiatives like Loop by TerraCycle are revolutionizing packaging. Loop offers products in reusable containers that can be returned, cleaned, and refilled. This system significantly reduces packaging waste and promotes a shift from single-use to reusable packaging.

Similarly, many supermarkets and food companies are adopting circular economy principles by minimizing food waste. For example, they are partnering with food rescue organizations to donate unsold but still edible food, which helps in reducing waste and addressing food insecurity.

These real-world examples demonstrate the practicality and replicability of circular economy principles across different industries. They highlight how businesses can not only reduce their environmental impact but also create innovative solutions that can be beneficial economically and socially. By showcasing successful implementations, these examples can inspire and guide other companies and industries to adopt circular economy practices.

Role of Individuals and Communities in the Circular Economy

Individual Contribution to the Circular Economy

Individuals have a significant role in shaping a sustainable future through their everyday choices and actions. Engaging in conscious consumerism is a key starting point; this means opting for products that are not only durable and repairable but also made from recycled or sustainable materials. Such choices can create a ripple effect, encouraging more sustainable production practices.

Proper disposal and recycling habits also form a cornerstone of individual contribution. Segregating waste, composting organic matter, and ensuring recyclables are clean and correctly sorted can profoundly impact the efficiency of recycling processes.

Moreover, the ethos of reuse and repair can be adopted in daily life. Instead of discarding items at the first sign of wear and tear, considering repair options or buying second-hand and refurbished products can significantly reduce waste.

Supporting businesses that align with circular economy principles is another powerful way individuals can contribute. Patronizing these businesses sends a strong message about consumer values and preferences, encouraging more companies to adopt sustainable strategies.

Finally, individuals can become advocates for the circular economy. By raising awareness and educating others, they can help foster a broader understanding and acceptance of these crucial practices.

Role of Communities and Local Governments

Communities and local governments are pivotal in creating an environment that supports and promotes circular economy practices. They can lead the charge by establishing efficient local recycling programs that are accessible and accommodate a diverse range of materials. This makes it easier and more convenient for residents to participate in recycling efforts.

Community-based initiatives like repair cafes and tool libraries can be nurtured, providing shared spaces for people to repair and reuse items. These initiatives not only reduce waste but also strengthen community bonds.

Educational campaigns spearheaded by local governments can enlighten residents about the circular economy's importance. These campaigns can offer practical advice on how to participate and contribute effectively, thereby fostering a community-wide shift towards sustainability.

Moreover, local governments can play a significant role in supporting circular economy businesses. This can be achieved through grants, incentives, and policies that favor sustainable business practices. Additionally, implementing regulations that require or incentivize sustainable practices, such as extended producer responsibility, can have a substantial impact on product lifecycle management.

Investing in infrastructure is also critical. Development of facilities for the collection, recycling, and processing of materials is essential for the practical implementation of circular economy principles.

By actively engaging both individuals and communities in the transition towards a circular economy, a collaborative and powerful force for sustainability is created. This collective approach ensures that the benefits of the circular economy—encompassing environmental protection, economic growth, and social development—are realized at every level of society.

Outlook

The circular economy represents a transformative approach, diverging from traditional linear models of production and consumption. Centered on principles of reducing waste, extending product life cycles, and regenerating natural systems, it offers a pathway towards sustainable economic development while addressing critical environmental challenges like climate change and resource depletion.

Key to this model are the core principles of reduce, reuse, and recycle, which together form a restorative and regenerative approach. Businesses in various industries, from fashion to electronics and food, have started implementing these principles, showcasing practical and replicable models of the circular economy in action.

Individuals and communities also play a significant role in this transition. Through conscious consumer choices, proper waste management, and support for sustainable practices, they can drive the demand for and success of circular economy models. Local governments and communities can further this by establishing supportive policies, educational initiatives, and recycling programs.

Looking ahead, the circular economy is poised for growth, with digital technologies, sustainable design, and cross-sector collaborations shaping its future. This evolution brings optimism, underscoring the importance of proactive engagement in sustainable practices for a more resilient and environmentally conscious world.

Periodical and Internet Sources Bibliography

The following articles have been selected to supplement the diverse views presented in this chapter.

Naman Bajaj, "Intention Over Impulse: 6 Tips to Avoid Overconsumption When Shopping Online," Commons, September 13, 2023. www.thecommons.earth/blog/intention-over-impulse-tips-to-avoid-overconsumption-when-shopping-online.

Peter Berg, David Feber, Anna Granskog, Daniel Nordigården, and Suku Ponkshe, "The Drive Toward Sustainability in Packaging—Beyond the Quick Wins," McKinsey & Company, January 30, 2020. www.mckinsey.com/industries/packaging-and-paper/our-insights/the-drive-toward-sustainability-in-packaging-beyond-the-quick-wins.

Patrick Hartmann, Aitor Marcosa, Juana Castro, and Vanessa Apaolaza, "Perspectives: Advertising and Climate Change – Part of the Problem or Part of the Solution?," International Journal of Advertising, October 24, 2022. www.tandfonline.com/doi/full/10.1080/02650487.2022.2140963.

Andrew J. Hoffman, "The Next Phase of Business Sustainability," Stanford Social Innovation Review, Spring 2018. ssir.org/articles/entry/the_next_phase_of_business_sustainability#.

Dana Miranda, "Without Restriction, How Do You Avoid Overconsumption?," Healthy Rich, February 12, 2024. www.healthyrich.co/p/avoid-overconsumption.

Georgia Meyers, "Why Do We Over-Consume?," Dover Crimsonian, September 27, 2024. dovercrimsonian.com/11815/opinion/why-do-we-over-consume-products/.

Halina Szejnwald Brown and Philip Vergragt, "From Consumerism to Wellbeing: Toward a Cultural Transition?," Journal of Cleaner Production, May 2015. www.researchgate.net/publication/276465574_From_Consumerism_to_Wellbeing_Toward_a_Cultural_Transition.

Madeleine Vollebregt, Ruth Mugge, Carina Thürridl, and Willemijn van Dolen, "Reducing without Losing: Reduced Consumption and Its Implications for Well-Being," Sustainable Production and Consumption, March 2024. www.sciencedirect.com/science/article/pii/S2352550923002981.

For Further Discussion

Chapter One

1. What role does consumerism currently play in modern life?
2. How does consumerism make life easier? How does it make life harder?
3. Do you believe consumerism can be classified as either good or bad?

Chapter Two

1. How do governments encourage overconsumption?
2. Do consumers and corporations have equal or unequal responsibility for reducing overconsumption?
3. What are some ways the rich can reduce their consumption?

Chapter Three

1. Is conscious consumerism enough to address the problem of overconsumption?
2. What role do companies play in addressing this problem?
3. Do you think it's possible to reduce our consumption?

Chapter Four

1. Does implementing a circular economy solve the problem of overconsumption or just change how it looks?
2. Why is it so hard to get people to change their attitudes about the economy?
3. In what ways are young people promoting change?

Organizations to Contact

The editors have compiled the following list of organizations concerned with the issues debated in this book. The descriptions are derived from materials provided by the organizations. All have publications or information available for interested readers. The list was compiled on the date of publication of the present volume; the information provided here may change. Be aware that many organizations take several weeks or longer to respond to inquiries, so allow as much time as possible.

Consumers International

70 White Lion Street
London, UK N1 9PP
Phone: +44 20 7226 6663
e-mail: consint@consint.org
Website: www.consumersinternational.org

Consumers International works to amplify the voices of consumers on the global stage, ensuring they receive the attention they deserve. The organization focuses on shaping policies and business practices that prioritize consumers' needs and rights in order to create an international marketplace that is fair, safe, and sustainable for everyone participating in it.

Cradle to Cradle Products Innovation Institute

2443 Fillmore Street, Suite 380-1625
San Francisco, CA 94115
Website: c2ccertified.org

This organization is a leader in the shift from a linear to a circular economy. It focuses on ensuring that products are designed with the environment in mind. It partners with businesses to improve product design and manufacturing practices. The organization also evaluates whether materials are safe for both people and the planet and encourages companies to prioritize reuse over disposal. Products that meet its strict environmental and health standards earn a special certification label that consumers can look for.

Earth911

3481 Plano Pkwy
The Colony, TX 75056
Website: earth911.com

Earth911 gives people information about how and where to recycle a wide range of items, including electronics and common household goods. In addition, the organization publishes helpful articles and resources on topics such as cutting down on waste, conserving energy, and making smarter, more eco-friendly purchasing decisions.

Green America

1612 K Street NW, Suite 1000
Washington, DC 20006
Phone: (800) 584-7336
Website: www.greenamerica.org

Green America is a nonprofit organization that has been working since 1982 to create a society that is both environmentally sustainable and socially just. The organization works to address social and environmental issues by encouraging people to use their economic power—as consumers, investors, employees, and business leaders—to drive positive change.

Plastic Pollution Coalition

4401A Connecticut Avenue NW, #143
Washington, DC 20008
Phone: (323) 936-3010
e-mail: donate@plasticpollutioncoalition.org
Website: www.plasticpollutioncoalition.org

The Plastic Pollution Coalition is a nonprofit organization that advocates for environmentally friendly alternatives to plastic. Through public education efforts, the organization raises awareness about the risks of plastic pollution. Its campaigns highlight the problems with single-use plastics and encourage people to shift toward more sustainable habits. It also collaborates with businesses to explore packaging solutions that are less wasteful and more eco-conscious.

Project Just

40 Worth Street, Suite 303
New York, NY 10013
e-mail: info@projectjust.com
website: www.projectjust.com

Project Just helps shoppers learn more about the supply chain practices of brands so they can become conscious consumers. The website reports on brands' labor conditions, environmental impact, and other factors that can help consumers shop at places that align with their values.

The Story of Stuff Project

1442 A Walnut Street, #272
Berkeley, CA 94709
Phone: (510) 883-1055
e-mail: info@storyofstuff.org
Website: storyofstuff.org

This nonprofit organization produces educational videos to raise awareness about the consequences of excessive consumption and the importance of adopting more sustainable habits. The group also partners with local communities and advocacy organizations to push for better product design. Their goal is to support systems where items are built to last, can be repaired or recycled, and cause less harm to the environment throughout their life cycle.

Bibliography of Books

Lara Barnes. *Green Living: Simple & Affordable Ways to Be Eco-Friendly.* Self-published, 2025.

Magnus Boström. *The Social Life of Unsustainable Mass Consumption.* Lanham, MD: Lexington Books, 2023.

Richard Denniss. *Curing Affluenza: How to Buy Less Stuff and Save the World.* Roseville, MN: Between the Lines, 2018.

Ferne Edwards. *Food Resistance Movements : Journeying Through Alternative Food Networks.* Singapore: Palgrave Macmillan, 2023.

Leila Fataar and Edward Pilkington. *Culture-Led Brands: Drive Growth, Build Resilience and Cultivate Resonance.* London, UK: Kogan Page, 2025.

Kristine H. Harper. *Anti-Trend: Resilient Design and the Art of Sustainable Living.* Novato, CA: Goff Books, 2021.

Naomi Klein. *This Changes Everything.* New York, NY: Simon & Schuster, 2014.

Frances Moore Lappe. *Diet for a Small Planet: The Book That Started a Revolution in the Way Americans Eat.* New York, NY: Ballantine Books, 1991.

Oliver Shaw. *The Rise of Consumerism: Economic Change in Post-War America.* Historia Magna, 2025.

Index

A

accommodation-sharing services, 121
addiction, 22
advertising, 68, 72, 79, 85–86, 109, 119, 143,
agriculture, 56, 74, 92, 94, 156
Apple, 163
anxiety, 16, 53, 55, 59–60
aviation, 82

B

biodiversity, 34, 74, 89, 92, 160
budget, 33, 38

C

capitalism, 16, 32, 72, 77, 131
Chinese culture, 42
choice editing, 84
circular economy, 105, 135–137, 155–166
climate change, 79–83, 85–86, 88–89, 96, 107–108, 113, 115–116, 156, 160, 166
conscious consumerism, 119, 120, 122–123, 164, 166
conservation of resources (COR) theory, 36–37, 41, 160
consumer
  effectiveness, 36, 42–43, 45–47
  exploitation, 31
  stress, 28–29, 32–41, 43–44, 57
contraception, 87–88, 90–91
Corporate Social Responsibility (CSR), 96–100
COVID-19 pandemic, 32–37, 42, 79–80, 83–84, 96–97, 99, 128–129, 134

D

daily needs, 38–39
dairy, 76–77, 83
deforestation, 74, 89
Dell, 163
depopulation, 75
depression, 16, 25, 53, 55
diets, 57, 76, 83
divorce, 27

E

Easterlin Paradox, 18–19, 23
e-commerce, 128
economic development, 156, 161, 166
economic growth, 68, 112–114, 116, 130, 159–160, 165

emissions, 74, 77, 80–83, 85, 88, 91, 107–109, 114–115, 127–129, 136, 158, 160
environment, 22, 26, 29, 34–35, 38, 41–47, 54–58, 60–61, 68–70, 72, 74, 76–78, 80–82, 86, 88, 90–93, 96, 105–107, 109, 113–116, 120–121, 123, 132–133, 139, 155–157, 159–161, 163–166
e-waste, 163
extinction, 70, 75, 83, 89, 113

F

fast fashion, 117, 128
flying, 80, 82–83
food choices, 57–58
food production, 71
food waste, 71, 75, 77, 163
fossil fuels, 81, 91, 109, 116

G

global oil reserves, 73
Great Pacific Garbage Patch, 73, 75
greenhouse gases, 80–81, 88, 107–108, 114, 158, 160
green technology, 76, 93, 129
greenwashing, 106–109

H

H&M, 134, 162–163
happiness, 17–19, 21, 23, 25–27, 34, 39, 44, 47, 55, 119, 126
housing, 58, 83, 85, 89–90
human evolution, 20

I

indigenous people, 74
indulgence, 36, 42, 44–47
inequality, 68, 80–81, 113
innovation, 30, 58, 105, 122–123, 161

J

jobs, 30, 75, 93, 96, 128, 131, 160

L

landfills, 115, 121, 135, 158, 160
legislation, 77
Levi's, 133
livestock, 71, 85

M

manufacturing processes, 93, 121–122, 160
materialism, 17, 24–30, 55, 60, 128–129, 133
meat consumption, 71
meat production, 76

N

natural resource extraction, 74–75
natural selection, 56

O

oceans, 75, 127–128, 156
omnichannel retailing, 55
online shopping, 72, 143
over-extraction of resources, 74
overfishing, 75
overpopulation, 88–91, 93–94
overshoot day, 70–71

P

panic buying, 33–34
parental activity outsourcing, 29
Patagonia, 133, 162
plant-based products, 76–77, 83
plastic, 73, 75–76, 156, 159, 163
pollution, 70, 83, 85–86, 88, 90–91, 93, 107, 114, 126, 129, 156, 160
poor diet, 57
prefrontal cortex, 20–21
product acquisition, 26
psychological effects, 29
public transport, 84–85
purchasing power, 17, 19
pursuit of wealth, 26

R

recovery levels, 35–36, 39–41, 43–46
recycling, 107, 114, 121, 156–166
refurbishment, 136, 146, 158, 160–164
retail therapy, 17, 130
reusable containers, 76, 163
ride-sharing services, 121

S

second-hand products, 135–146, 163–164
self-control, 34, 38–39, 43–44, 58
self-esteem, 21–22, 55
smartphones, 16, 121, 127–128
social calculator, 21
social esteem, 22
social media, 55, 60, 79–80, 132, 144
social rejection, 60
social status, 16, 22, 60, 83, 119
stockpiling behavior, 33–34
sustainability, 69, 83, 85, 87–90, 93–96, 99, 105–109, 114–115, 120–123, 126, 140, 155, 165
SUVs, 25, 82–83, 85–86

T

taxes, 83–84
technological advances, 93
textiles industry, 117
Thunberg, Greta, 80, 83, 113, 116

trash islands, 73

U

unneeded consumption, 32–47

V

voluntary simplicity, 132

W

waste, 18, 31, 68, 70–73, 75, 77, 88, 90, 105, 109, 115, 121, 126, 136, 140, 156–161, 163–166
wildfires, 107
work engagement, 36, 40–41, 43, 45–46
WWF, 73, 75, 89

Z

Zara, 134